In the 1990s, psychologists began to systematically explore the contributions of spirituality to human wellbeing, but the importance of time in nature for young children's spiritual development remained a neglected topic. This book corrects that oversight, showing many ways that engaging with nature deepens children's spirituality—with benefits for children and the care and protection of the natural world—and suggesting activities to encourage these connections. Firmly grounded in research as well as experience in early childhood education, this book balances scholarship and practical recommendations with poetry, story and reflection.

–Louise Chawla, University of Colorado Boulder

Research has much to say about how nature enhances children's learning, health, mental health and environmental stewardship. Ruth Wilson persuades us that there is something more to it. By exploring "something" within the child (spirituality), within nature (sacredness), and within their relationship (reciprocity), Ruth Wilson deftly fills this gap.

–Cathy Jordan, PhD., Consulting Director of Research, Children & Nature Network

Ruth Wilson comprehensively draws on her many years of experience to "turn the tide" with this publication. Children's nature connections, spirituality and sustainability are woven together through research, reflections and stories offering much for readers to deeply consider and act upon. At a time when global climate change is pressing, we all need a spiritually restorative space, whatever that may be. The mandate here is for the adults in children's lives to create such spaces with children and to envision sustainable futures together.

–Dr Sue Elliott, University of New England, Australia

With clear explanations, a compelling framework and significant details are provided to meaningfully guide children in co-existing with the more-than-human world. This book transforms our thinking and offers a guide to transformations needed in early childhood education.
–Yash Bhagwanji, Ph.D., Florida Atlantic University; Editor, *International Journal of Early Childhood Environmental Education*

As a pioneer of early childhood nature-based education, Ruth Wilson has written a masterful and insightful new book that explores how spending time in the natural world can have a deep impact on children's developing spirituality. Weaving together fundamental children and nature research with heartfelt stories and personal reflections, this book provides a new look on an important topic that is more relevant today than ever.
–Patti Bailie, Ph.D., Associate Professor Emerita, University of Maine at Farmington; Co-author of *Partnering with Nature in Early Childhood* and *Evaluating Natureness*

Dr. Wilson hit it out of the ballpark yet again with another book that fills the reader with important information conveyed clearly, with elegance, grace and respect. Taking on the topic of spirituality in childhood is brave. Her capacity to connect nature and spirituality for both children and adults expands the traditional view of what many equate with what is spiritual. Dr. Wilson's strength, among many, is making the clear link between biophilia and spirituality feel like a natural part of childhood and youth. This book demystifies the concept of spirituality and puts it into the hands of adults to provide children with opportunities and affordances in nature to nourish their souls. A world in which children can be their best self-thanks to healthy doses of

nature might just be the world in which future generations and our planet can flourish. And what a gift that will be.
—Amy Wagenfeld, Department of Landscape Architecture, University of Washington; co-author *Nature-Based Allied Health Practice | The Nature of Inclusive Play*

I read Ruth Wilson's book word for word. I was spellbound by the depth and sensitivity given to the interrelationship between nature, spirituality, and humans, especially young humans. In this book, Ruth shares her insights that come from her many years of experience working with children and educators, as well as her personal love of nature and sense of wonder that leads to dreams for a better tomorrow.
—Deb Schein, Researcher, Author and Loose Parts Play specialist

This beautiful book made my heart and my soul sing! Ruth Wilson provides such thoughtful language and insight that I will continue to reference again and again. From reflections on relational spirituality to considerations of spirituality in nature play and in environmental justice, Ruth weaves together a rich, multi-layered tapestry of evocative research and grounded experience. I want to put this book into the hands of every educator I know, regardless of whether they are a religious educator, environmental educator or early childhood educator.
—Chaplain Dave Becker, Unitarian Universalist Minister, Interfaith Chaplain, Educator, and Activist

Nature and Spirituality During the Early Years

This practical and easy-to-read guide shows you how to integrate nature connectedness and spiritual development into your early childhood teaching, whether in a nature-based forest program or a more traditional one. It uses a research-based framework to illustrate ways nature and spirituality can contribute to quality of life during the early childhood years and beyond. Detailing favourable conditions for supporting children's connectedness to nature and spiritual development—including positive relationships with adults and peers, violence-free environments, and respect for other living things—the book emphasizes the idea of children's whole-body engagement, challenging the idea that spirituality is relevant to the mind and spirit only. This guidebook is essential reading for all early childhood educators, program directors, families, and anyone working with children and young people.

Ruth Wilson, Ph.D., has been an educator and teacher educator for over 30 years and has devoted most of her career to connecting young children with nature. She recently worked as curator for the Children & Nature Network Research Library, an online resource of scientific literature relating to children and nature.

Other Eye on Education Books
Available from Routledge
(www.routledge.com/eyeoneducation)

Optimizing Early Auditory Development for Communication and Education
Strategies for Ages 0–8
Kimberly A. Boynton and Darah J. Regal

A New Vision for Early Childhood
Rethinking Our Relationships with Young Children
Noah Hichenberg

Unpacking Privilege in the Elementary Classroom
A Guide to Race and Inequity for White Teachers
Jacquelynne Boivin and Kevin McGowan

Reimagining the Role of Teachers in Nature-based Learning
Helping Children be Curious, Confident, and Caring
Rachel Larimore and Claire Warden

Promoting Language and Early Literacy Development
Practical Insights from a Parent Researcher
Pamela Beach

Teaching Higher-Order Thinking to Young Learners, K–3
How to Develop Sharp Minds for the Disinformation Age
Steffen Saifer

Nature and Spirituality During the Early Years
Ruth Wilson

Nature and Spirituality During the Early Years

Ruth Wilson

Taylor & Francis Group

NEW YORK AND LONDON

Designed cover image: Getty images

First published 2026
by Routledge
605 Third Avenue, New York, NY 10158

and by Routledge
4 Park Square, Milton Park, Abingdon, Oxon, OX14 4RN

Routledge is an imprint of the Taylor & Francis Group, an informa business

© 2026 Ruth Wilson

The right of Ruth Wilson to be identified as author of this work has been asserted in accordance with sections 77 and 78 of the Copyright, Designs and Patents Act 1988.

All rights reserved. No part of this book may be reprinted or reproduced or utilised in any form or by any electronic, mechanical, or other means, now known or hereafter invented, including photocopying and recording, or in any information storage or retrieval system, without permission in writing from the publishers.

Trademark notice: Product or corporate names may be trademarks or registered trademarks, and are used only for identification and explanation without intent to infringe.

ISBN: 978-1-032-93614-7 (hbk)
ISBN: 978-1-032-93612-3 (pbk)
ISBN: 978-1-003-56671-7 (ebk)

DOI: 10.4324/9781003566717

Typeset in Palatino
by SPi Technologies India Pvt Ltd (Straive)

For the oneness of the Earth

Contents

Meet the Author xiii
List of Boxes... xiv
List of Tables xv
Introduction: Soul-Making.. xvi

1 At Home in Nature... 1

2 Who Has Seen the Wind? 12

3 Experiences in and with Nature.................................23

4 Spiritual Benefits 37

5 Spiritual Roots...48

6 Trail Guide 65

7 A Proposed Framework 79

8 Nature Play...92

9 Mindfulness in Nature 107

10 Philosophical Thinking...122

11 Wonder, Aesthetics, and the Creative Arts.....................135

12 Stories, Poems, and Storytelling 151

Afterword: There Was a Time........................167

References *169*

Meet the Author

Ruth Wilson, Ph.D., has been an educator and teacher educator for over 30 years and has devoted most of her career to connecting young children with nature. She recently worked as curator for the Children & Nature Network Research Library, an online resource of scientific literature relating to children and nature. She also serves as a consulting editor for the *International Journal of Early Childhood Environmental Education* and has written numerous articles for academic journals. Ruth has several published books, including *Special Educational Needs in the Early Years* (Routledge 1998, 2003), *Nature and Young Children* (Routledge 2007, 2012, 2018), and *Naturally Inclusive* (Gryphon House 2022). Ruth has conducted a number of online seminars and has given presentations at professional conversations. Ruth lives in New Mexico, where she enjoys hiking in the land of enchantment.

Boxes

1.1	Reflections: What We Yearn For	3
1.2	Research Note: Nature/Spirituality/Happiness Link	6
1.3	Implications for Practice: Appreciative Interactions	10
2.1	Implications for Practice: Playing with Words and Ideas	17
2.2	Research Note: Teacher Reflections and Practices	21
3.1	Reflections: Learning in and with the Weather	30
3.2	Research Note: Co-Habiting vs. Domination	32
3.3	Implications for Practice: Playful Experiences in the Forest	35
4.1	Reflections: A Spiritual Moment	38
4.2	Research Note: Awe in Nature Heals	41
4.3	Suggestions: "Go Green" with Peace Education	46
5.1	Suggestions: Know Your Why	52
5.2	Research Note: Nature Play and Sustainability	57
5.3	Reflections: Education as if People and Planet Mattered	61
6.1	Reflections: One with Nature	71
6.2	Suggestions: Promoting Children's Agency	73
7.1	Reflections: Ecological Self/Spiritual Self	82
7.2	Research Note: High-Impact Experiences	87
8.1	Research Note: Nature Play Remembered	95
8.2	Suggestions: Supporting Spiritual Development	105
9.1	Research Note: Mindfulness and Connectedness to Nature	108
9.2	Reflections: Rhythm	120
10.1	Reflections: *Plato, Not Prozac!*	125
10.2	Suggestions: Guidelines for Fostering Philosophical Thinking	134
11.1	Reflections: Aesthetics and a Sense of Wonder	137
11.2	Program Spotlight: Running Wild	149
12.1	Reflections: Learning from the Book of Nature	159
12.2	Suggestions: Literacy Outdoors	164

Tables

6.1 Contrasting Priorities in the Human/Nature
    Relationship   67
7.1 Framework for Promoting the Spiritual Dimensions
    of Young Children's Connectedness to Nature   90

Introduction

Soul-Making

The poet John Keats once referred to the world in which we live as a "vale of soul-making" and noted how this view differs from the more common image of the world as a "vale of tears." People who think of the world as a "vale of tears" tend to believe that our role in this life is to work for redemption and eventually earn our way to a better place. Such thinking, according to Keats, is misguided and superstitious. He suggests relating to the Earth as a "vale of soul-making", and, in doing so, tap into "a system of Spirit-creation" (Keats 1819).

Both personal experiences and a rich body of research support the idea of the Earth – or the world of nature — as a "vale of soul-making." Scientists such as the American biologist and naturalist E.O. Wilson recognize that Earth is the "birthplace of our spirit" and that nature has helped to shape our souls (Wilson 1992). The term "biophilia" is sometimes used in reference to what we experience as nature's gravitational pull on our spirits and on our souls. This pull is more than a casual affinity or attraction (Wilson 2006). It's a part of our soulfulness.

What the poet Keats refers to as a "vale of soul-making" and what scientists refer to as "biophilia" are overlapping ideas. Both concepts reference nature as a key source of inspiration and nourishment for the human spirit. Young children seem to sense this feature of nature intuitively. Until they're taught differently, young children tend to be in tune with the soul-making aspects of the human–Earth relationship. Unfortunately, what they see and hear around them often draws children into a more materialistic and consumeristic relationship with nature. They begin to view nature as a resource to be used or as an "other" to be dismissed. This shift from affinity to dismissal can happen during the early childhood years. The framework presented in this book is designed to turn the tide: to make nature connectedness—especially the spiritual dimensions of this connectedness—a focus of a young child's life.

While there has been tremendous growth over the past several years in the number and types of initiatives connecting (or re-connecting) children to nature, I sense the need for "something more." This "something more", I believe, relates to something within the child, within nature, and within the relationship between the two.

The "something" within the child is spirituality; within nature, sacredness; and within the relationship, reciprocity. Each of these "somethings" is addressed in this book as a component of a framework for promoting the spiritual dimensions of young children's connectedness to nature. At the core of this framework is the idea of engagement with nature as a soul-making experience.

The book is based on two basic premises: (1) spirituality is an integral part of a child's holistic development, and (2) nature connectedness includes a spiritual component. A major concept highlighted throughout the book relates to the critical need to revive humanity's spiritual connection to nature as a way to address the environmental crisis and to enrich our experience of life on Earth. While the book is written primarily for educators, mental health therapists, program developers, and other adults working to promote the holistic development of young children, it will also be of interest to readers looking for more information about the spirituality and nature connection.

This book is not a curriculum guide for nature-based learning, nor does it offer specific activities to do with young children to promote spirituality. What it does offer are some research-based ideas and guidelines for promoting an often-overlooked area of children's connectedness with the rest of the natural world. This is the area of spirituality. Rather than suggesting specific activities or strategies that might be used to support children's spiritual development, the book offers some guidelines for evaluating different ideas and approaches. The framework outlined in this book can enhance and complement existing educational guides and community programs.

The first part of the book (Chapters 1, 2, and 3) considers the main players involved in the discussion: nature, children, and the relationship between the two. Chapters 4 and 5 discuss how highlighting the spiritual dimensions of connectedness to nature benefits children, society, and the environment. Chapter 6 addresses some of the major facilitators and inhibitors to integrating spirituality and nature in the daily lives of young children. Chapter 7 proposes a theoretical framework for doing so. The final section (Chapters 8 through 12) considers specific venues or pathways for implementing the proposed framework.

1

At Home in Nature

Human Connectedness to Nature

The recent growth of forest schools and nature-based preschools has been phenomenal. The reasons for this are varied, but the most compelling force behind this surge may relate to biophilia. We, as humans, are drawn to nature. Scientists have termed this yearning "biophilia" and defined it as an "innate tendency to affiliate with life and lifelike processes" (Wilson 2006, p. 63).

The word "biophilia" may be new to some people, yet the feeling associated with it isn't. We experience biophilia as an attraction to trees, flowers, streams, animals, and the many other natural features in the world around us. We may even experience biophilia as a sense of kinship with other living things (Wilson 2022).

E.O. Wilson, the scientist who popularized the concept of biophilia, refers to Earth as the birthplace of our spirit and nature as an entity that has helped to shape our souls. Our "spiritual roots", he says, "extend deep into the natural world through still mostly hidden channels of mental development" (Wilson 2006, p. 12). Stephen Kellert, who worked with Wilson in pioneering the theory of biophilia, explains how our human dependence on nature reaches far beyond a reliance upon physical sustenance. We have, he says, a craving for the aesthetic, intellectual, and spiritual benefits nature has to offer. Kellert describes how immersing ourselves in nature takes us to a place where we can find "spiritual fulfillment and a life of meaning and purpose" (Kellert 2012, p. 103). He also notes how biophilia includes both "the quest for empirical understanding and the pursuit of spiritual meaning" (Kellert 2007, p. 28).

Biologist Clemens Arvay – whose research focused on a scientific and spiritual exploration of the healing bond between humans and nature – echoes the work of Kellert and Wilson. Arvay (2018a) refers to the forest as a "space for souls" (p. 48) and explains how when we are in a nature-rich setting, "biophilic forces within us drive us to be close to life and growth processes" (Arvay 2018b, p. 70).

Wilson was a biologist whose work in entomology led him to become the world authority on ants. Kellert was a social ecologist who pioneered the concept and framework for biophilic design (an approach to constructing places that connect people and nature). Arvay was an Austrian scientist whose research in health ecology led to the science of eco-psychosomatics (a study of the close connections between body, mind, and nature or between natural habitats and human health). While the research interests and professional accomplishments of these three scientists differ widely, they each recognized a spiritual dimension to the human connection to nature. Individuals from other disciplines have done so as well and include naturalists Diane Ackerman and Ann Zwinger, literature scholars Scott Russell Sanders and Scott Slovic, poets Mary Oliver and Wendell Berry, journalists J.B. MacKinnon and Richard Louv, psychologists James Hillman and Cynthia Frantz, and philosophers Max Oelschlaeger and David Abram.

There are, of course, many other scholars and writers who have identified strong connections between spirituality and human connectedness to nature. The emergence of ecopsychology in the 1990s is another indication of interest in understanding these connections. Theodore Roszak, a recognized scholar in the field of ecopsychology, notes how living in balance with nature is an essential component of our emotional and spiritual well-being (Roszak 1992).

A rise in the publication of nature memoirs – such as *The Wild Places* by Robert Macfarland and *Braiding Sweetgrass* by Robin Wall Kimmerer – is another indication that people from all walks of life are looking for something below the surface of humans' physical connectedness to nature. What we all seem to be yearning for are deeper and more soul-ful connections with the world around us.

BOX 1.1   REFLECTIONS: WHAT WE YEARN FOR

For hundreds of years, biophilia has served us well. We lived close to and learned important lessons from the rest of the natural world. The experience of living close to the natural world, however, is diminishing rapidly.

Today, we live most of our lives in built versus natural environments. We look to science, engineering, and mass production to meet our basic needs and to feed our enormous appetite for dominion or control (Kellert 2012). This shift comes with a cost. While we may *think* that our lives are improving and expanding, we may *feel* a sense of diminishment. We may be able to travel around the world in less than 24 hours, communicate with people across the globe in a matter of seconds, and eat food grown thousands of miles from our home and yet feel a sense of uneasiness about our grounding on planet Earth. Our spirits yearn for more than speed, comfort, convenience, and entertainment. We yearn for connectedness and purpose.

Nature is our natural habitat. Other living creatures – both plants and animals – thrive best in their native environments. Their natural habitats provide the support they need to function effectively in an interdependent web of existence. We, as humans, "will never be truly satisfied, or fulfilled if we live apart and alienated from the environment from which we evolved" (Kellert 2012, p. x). We need nature to nurture our senses, intellect, emotions, and spirit. This is true for individuals and for society.

Biophilia may be an inborn characteristic of humans, but for our biophilic tendencies to flourish, we need nature-rich experiences and the support of others. Nature is more than a resource or entertainment for humans; it's a necessity for our physical, mental, and spiritual flourishing.

The gifts of nature are abundant, providing nourishment for every aspect of our beings. While we've become quite adept at accessing the physical and mental gifts of the natural world, we tend to be less appreciative of the spiritual gifts. For our own well-being and the well-being of the Earth, our spiritual connections with nature need to be recognized and supported. Ignoring biophilia – or allowing biophilia to diminish as a force in our lives – will not only chip away at the quality of our lives but also be detrimental to the well-being of the other-than-human elements of the Earth.

Perhaps what's desperately needed at this time in human history is a transformation of consciousness. Eckhart Tolle in *A New Earth* (2005) speaks to this need. Tolle notes how "most people don't inhabit a living reality, but a conceptualized one" (p. 37). He also describes how human consciousness is currently trapped in a state of dysfunction, based on ego-driven thoughts and desires. In our search for cleverness, he says, we tend to lose wisdom along the way.

Perhaps it's time to acknowledge that wisdom is far deeper than thought and that the unnecessary frames (and constraints) we've placed around our thinking and feeling are interfering with a more joyful way of living. Perhaps it's time to intentionally engage with nature through our senses and emotions – not just through our thoughts and economic endeavours.

Children and Nature

The phenomenal growth in forest schools and nature-based preschools around the world may also be related to a greater awareness of the many benefits of frequent interactions with the world of nature. An impressive body of research shows that connecting children to nature during the early years of life has many long-term benefits. These benefits apply to all areas of child development. The online Research Library developed and maintained by the Children & Nature Network (https://research.childrenandnature.org/) includes over 1500 summaries of studies documenting the many benefits of access to nature for children of all ages. Almost 500 of these studies include children between birth and five years of age.

Every child has a life force that sustains and animates their being. This life force needs nourishment to grow. One critical source of nourishment is the Earth itself. Richard Louv (2006), in a passionate plea to connect children with nature, notes how their "mental, physical, and spiritual health depends upon it" (p. 3). Other scholars agree. Carol Ryff, a positive psychology researcher, for example, documents ways in which the power of nature nurtures human spirituality and well-being. She refers to the life force as "soul" and recognizes it as "a force that links us with meaning" (Ryff 2021, p. 11). Ryff highlights ways in which nature has inspired poetry, literature, art, and music. "These works", she says, "reveal that the natural world speaks to the human soul" (Ryff 2021, p. 1).

Louv (2006) acknowledges the difficulty in actually measuring the contribution of nature to the spiritual life of the child. This should not deter us, he says, from looking to nature as a source of spiritual nourishment. Louv follows his own advice by devoting an entire section of his book, *Last Child in the Woods*, to the spiritual benefits of nature for children. He refers to nature as a "spiritual necessity" (p. 285) and highlights the fact that most of children's transcendent experiences occur in nature. Research supports this assertion. Tobin Hart (2006), for example, cites numerous studies indicating that "time in nature is the most common catalyst for moments of wonder" (p. 165). And wonder, as many of us know, is a characteristic and pathway to spirituality.

Sadly, as Louv (2006) notes, some religions and faith-based organizations aren't comfortable with the idea of looking to nature for spiritual nourishment. Their concern tends to focus on animism – that is, attributing spirit or soul to other-than-human elements of nature. This concern, Louv (2006) says, "is perhaps one of the least acknowledged but more important barriers between children and nature" (p. 292). Wilson also addressed this concern. In *The Creation*, written as a letter to a Southern

Baptist pastor, Wilson (2006) explains how animistic views and "animistic sensibility" aren't incompatible with the beliefs of many faith-based organizations.

Today, there are indications that nature-based spirituality is becoming part of different religions across the globe (Taylor 2020). Some church groups sponsor nature camps for kids and encourage pro-environmental practices. Some offer nature-based preschools and engage youth in environmental activism. Pope Francis and other church leaders issued proclamations about the importance of care for the Earth (Wilson 2006).

While nature-based spirituality is growing within faith-based organizations, it is also becoming embedded in some educational programs outside of religions. SOL [Soulful Outdoor Learning] Forest School in New Mexico is one example of this. SOL engages children in frequent mindfulness practices, rituals, and routines in a forest school setting to help them "discover the solace, serenity, silence, and solitude that is offered in nature" (https://www.solforestschool.com/).

BOX 1.2   RESEARCH NOTE: NATURE/SPIRITUALITY/HAPPINESS LINK

The idea that nature engagement, spirituality, and well-being are positively linked is supported by a growing number of research studies. In one such study, people with higher levels of nature exposure reported better psychological well-being and scored higher on a scale of spirituality (Kamitsis & Francis 2013) than people with lower levels of nature exposure. These results are consistent with other research showing that nature can make an important contribution to people experiencing a sense of spirituality and life satisfaction (Lincoln 2000). While some of this research focuses on adults, a 2023 review of the literature on the impacts of nature connectedness focused specifically on children's well-being. The well-being benefits for children identified in this review were numerous and included "experiences of mindfulness or spirituality" (Arola et al. 2023, p. 4).

In another study (Holder et al. 2016), over a thousand children and youth completed a survey which included assessments of happiness, life satisfaction, religiosity, and spirituality. The spirituality assessment was based on the nature domain of spirituality, which focuses on an individual's connectedness to nature. Spirituality, as measured by the nature domain, was shown to be a strong predictor of children's life satisfaction and a moderate predictor of adolescents' happiness and life satisfaction.

Other research, too, links connectedness to nature and spirituality. In addition to identifying connectedness to nature as a domain of spirituality, it recognizes nature engagement as a pathway to spirituality (Barrera-Hernandez et al. 2020). A child encountering the beauty and wonder of nature may experience awe and feelings of joy. Such encounters – or spiritual moments – can foster other aspects of child development, such as perspective taking, enhanced social connections, life satisfaction, and a sense of well-being (Capaldi, Dopko & Zelenski 2014; Fretwell & Greig 2019).

Kinship and Identity

Unless taught otherwise, children seem to know that nature is their natural habitat, that nature is a place where they can thrive. Nature, for children, is often a source of comfort, a place of discovery and delight, and a habitat where they can be their most authentic selves. Children often experience a sense of wonder, joy, and awe as they explore the world of nature. These spiritual or "soul-making" experiences tend to foster a sense of oneness or kinship with the rest of the natural world.

While kinship in some contexts refers to a blood relationship, it can also be experienced as an emotional relationship. When it is viewed as a blood relationship, the emphasis is on "of the same kind." When it is viewed as an emotional relationship, the emphasis is on a common world – a world to be shared with all other creatures (Wilson 2022). This understanding is a basic component of eco-spirituality and crucial to the healthy development of a child's ecological identity.

"Ecological identity" refers to one's connections with the rest of the natural world (Wilson 2018). A healthy ecological identity includes such positive environmental attitudes and values as appreciating and caring for the natural world. While there are overlaps between the concepts of an environmental ethic and an ecological identity, there are slight differences between the two. An environmental ethic is a guide for *what we do* in interacting with the natural world. This guide is based on a moral relationship. An ecological identity, on the other hand, focuses on *who we are* and how we view ourselves in relation to the rest of the natural world (Wilson 2018). Viewing ourselves as closely related to other living things on planet Earth forms the basis of a kinship relationship.

For many indigenous people, the kinship relationship means viewing "both themselves and nature as part of an extended ecological family that shares ancestry and origins" (Salmon 2000, p. 1327). According to this view, human relatives include all the natural elements of an ecosystem. This view – referred to as "kincentric ecology" – includes the understanding that the interactions between humans and the other-than-humans impact the life around them and that if humans fail to recognize "their role in the complexities of life in a place, the life suffers and loses its sustainability" (Salmon 2000, p. 1327). Kincentric ecology thus suggests that a spiritual foundation is a necessary component of sustainability. This idea is discussed further in Chapter 5.

A number of factors influence how a child's ecological identity develops, including where the child lives and plays, interactions with adults and peers, educational and cultural experiences, and extent of engagement with the natural world. One of the most important factors in developing a healthy ecological identity is the opportunity to experience frequent positive interactions with nature during childhood (Broom 2017; Williams & Chawla 2016).

Early Experiences and Ways of Knowing

Rachel Sebba, a researcher whose work focuses on children and their environments, investigated possible connections between the meaning given to the memory of past surroundings and the physical characteristics of those surroundings. Her research indicates that many adults identify the outdoors as the most significant factor in their childhood (Sebba 1991). Other researchers report similar findings (Broom 2017; Cagle 2018; Howell & Allen 2019; Hsu 2017)

Sebba's research indicates that children's way of knowing the natural world involves more physical interaction and sensory absorption than detached or analytical observation. She notes how, for children, perception often conducts thought, whereas, with adults, thought tends to conduct perception. In other words, by the time we're adults, we tend to see the world and think about the world in relation to models handed to us. Children's thoughts, on the other hand, aren't clouded or shaped by previously formed models of the world. Children tend to experience the environmental features of the outdoors as "active factors" rather than merely background for human activities (Sebba 1991).

Children take in the world of nature through their senses and observations of what happens as they interact with it. Annie Dillard (1974) notes how children "have highly developed 'input systems,' admitting all data indiscriminately" (p. 91). Young children don't screen out information they receive through their senses based on what is socially acceptable or what they've been told to believe. They keep their eyes and minds open to what they actually experience.

Children come to know a tree, for example, by being in its presence, interacting with it, and developing a relationship with it. The child's experience goes beyond "learning about a tree" to gaining insights into the essence – or "treeness" – of the tree. Thus, it's not unusual for a child to know a tree as a giver of gifts, a protector, and a friend.

Experiences with nature during childhood can lead to the development of deep emotional connections with nature that remain through adulthood. Such experiences can lay the foundation for a lifelong commitment to caring for nature (Chawla 1999; Tanner 1980). Such experiences can also impact an individual's mental health and well-being over time (Jimenez et al. 2020). Louise Chawla's research on memories of childhood experiences provides an example of how special childhood places – especially places in natural environments – can enrich our lives both in the moment and over time. She describes such memories as "radioactive jewels buried within us, emitting energy across the years of our life" (Chawla 1990, p. 18).

Conclusion

The way children view and interact with the natural world tends to be qualitatively different from adults. "They sense the magic of life, and sometimes talk about things like rocks and clouds as alive" (Beery, Chawla & Levin 2020, p. 17). The fact that young children sense the "magic of life" and engage in magical thinking is something that we, as adults, would do well to respect and support. "Magic is an exploratory experience that shapes the earliest forms of science and knowledge production. Magic … facilitates interrogation and fosters a desire to understand" (Armijo-Cabrera 2025, p. 16).

An appreciation of how children view the world of nature calls for a shift in the fields of child development and early childhood education. This shift should include greater attention to ways in which the natural world and children's interactions with it contribute to their holistic development. Adults working with young children would do well to recognize and value children's perspectives and ways of interacting with nature. They would also do well to recognize and promote the spiritual dimensions of children's connectedness to nature.

BOX 1.3   IMPLICATIONS FOR PRACTICE: APPRECIATIVE INTERACTIONS

Increasing the amount of time children spend outdoors is one way to deepen their connectedness to nature. What they do when they're outdoors, however, also makes a difference. Interactions with nature tend to fall within three categories: appreciative, consumptive, and destructive (Hoover 2021). Of these, appreciative interactions tend to be the most effective in promoting children's spiritual connections with nature.

Appreciative interactions allow for enjoyment of nature without causing harm. This doesn't mean that children should just be observing nature or that adults should be promoting a "hands-off" approach. Examples of appreciative interactions are walking barefoot through the grass or sand, collecting fallen leaves to create a three-dimensional work of art, and sprinkling water over dried moss to "wake it up." Some consumptive activities can also be appreciative, such as picking strawberries and enjoying them for lunch. With consumptive activities, however, attention needs to be paid to the impact on the environment.

Appreciative activities not only bring joy to the child but also increase the likelihood of stronger connections with nature and engagement in pro-environmental behaviours later in life (Hoover 2021). In fact, appreciative interactions reflect a coming together of sustainability and spirituality (Leal Filho et al. 2022). Here are other examples of appreciative nature-related activities for young children:

- Watering plants
- Feeding birds
- Lining a path with stones
- Drawing a tree
- Sorting natural materials (seeds, stones, sticks, etc.) by colour, size, or texture
- Floating natural materials (fallen leaves or bark, feathers, etc.) in a bucket or stream of water
- Fingerpainting with mud

2

Who Has Seen the Wind?

Spirituality and Religion

Interest in childhood spirituality has been on the rise for quite some time, yet it's not regularly addressed in the early childhood literature (Adams, Bull & Maynes 2016; Hart 2006). In the wider world, however, scholars in other disciplines have formed interest groups and organized professional meetings and conferences exploring issues relating to childhood spirituality. Reasons behind such initiatives are varied. Some people feel that the beliefs, values, and commitments associated with religion are no longer recognized by the younger generation as guideposts for how to live in a complex world and that spirituality may fill this gap. Others may feel that traditional religions have become irrelevant, and perhaps even divisive, in a multicultural society. They may, thus, look to spirituality versus religion as an avenue for guiding children in their journey toward becoming caring and contributing members of society.

Yet the lack of attention to spirituality in the lives of young children is due, in part, to the fact that spirituality has been inextricably linked with religion (Adams, Bull & Maynes 2016) and considered to be "a thoroughly private, self-enclosed affair" (Hay 2000, p. 39). By the age of ten, children seem to be aware of a social taboo against expressing or recognizing the spiritual dimension of human experience. The resulting "forgetfulness of spirituality" has now become "a socially constructed amnesia" (Hay 2000, p. 40).

Meaning of Spirituality

Of course, it's hard to talk about children's spirituality without coming to a clear understanding about the meaning of spirituality generally. Spirituality, for some, is rooted in a sense of the sacred and/or a search for the sacred. Others, however, may define spirituality without reference to a sacred or transcendent realm. They may see spirituality as a set of human qualities, which includes insight and an awareness of interconnections between persons and other life forms. This view is consistent with the idea that spirituality is something that we experience primarily through feelings of awe, gratitude, and mystery. Spirituality can also be perceived as "a developmental wellspring out of which emerges the pursuit of meaning, connectedness to others and the sacred, purpose, and contributions, each and all of which can be addressed by religion or other systems of ideas and beliefs" (Roehlkepartain et al. 2006, p. 5). This definition suggests that spirituality is a universal phenomenon, experienced by every human being, and that it can develop over time.

Differing ideas about the meaning of spirituality reflect the complexity and multidimensional nature of the phenomenon. Adding to the complexity is the understanding that the experience of spirituality may differ from person to person and from culture to culture. Spirituality may also take on different dimensions at different stages during one's life. While the research on spirituality is ongoing, findings consistent across multiple studies indicate that spirituality is innate and that its characteristics include a sense of awe, wonder, transcendent experiences, a search for meaning and purpose, self-knowledge, hope, love, and courage (Nye & Hay 1996; Ryff 2021).

In some ways, spirituality is "like the wind – though it might be experienced, observed, and described, it cannot be 'captured'" (Roehlkepartain et al. 2006, p. 6). Martin Buber, a German philosopher and theologian, offers a similar view. Spirit, he says, is "like the air in which you breathe" (Buber 1923/1970, p. 89). In spite of its fuzziness, "all definitions of spirituality in some way or another overlap each other" (Gellel 2018, p. 18). Different definitions of spirituality also indicate that spirituality integrates various aspects of what it means to be human.

Some of the research on spirituality comes from the health-related field. This research reflects a growing interest in connections between spirituality and quality of life and includes the understanding that spirituality is "an indispensable element for human flourishing" (Ellyatt 2024, p. 92).

Experiencing quality of life means more than the absence of illness or discomfort (Panzini et al. 2017). Quality of life is a presence, an overall feeling of well-being, allowing us to participate in and enjoy the events of life. The related research indicates that, without spirituality, quality of life and a sense of holistic well-being are compromised. It also indicates that engagement with nature contributes to both spirituality and quality of life (Hanson & Jones 2020; Heintzman 2009). Spiritual qualities promoted through nature engagement include personal fulfilment and pro-social behaviours such as cooperating, sharing, comforting, and offering help (Putra et al. 2020).

Children's Spirituality

In addition to a lack of clarity about what the term means, another reason why spirituality is often lacking in the early childhood literature is the idea that certain aspects of spirituality fall outside the framework of developmental theory. Some theories about cognitive development, for example, suggest that young children aren't intellectually mature enough to engage in meaningful reflection around issues such as self-awareness, identity, purpose, and interconnectedness (Hart 2006). This line of thinking is based on the mistaken belief that genuine spirituality requires abstract thinking and thus is a phenomenon experienced only by adults.

Scholars studying children's spirituality, however, note how elements of spirituality exist outside the domain of rational thought and are often experienced through wonder (Hart 2006). Even very young children – with limited ability to think and talk about spiritual concepts – have the potential for spiritual experiences, including an awareness of the sacred. They may also demonstrate an awareness of these experiences. For example, a preschool child may experience excitement and joy in seeing a rainbow. Later, this same child may draw a picture of a rainbow to depict something special that he or she experienced. The child's awareness about what was experienced while seeing the rainbow is a type of knowing that isn't dependent on a certain stage of cognitive development. The initial joy and excitement – and the remembrance of having those feelings – reflect elements of spirituality.

Scholars studying children's spirituality have identified various ways in which children demonstrate spiritual capacities (Adams, Bull & Maynes 2016; Giesenberg 2000; Hart 2006; Hay & Nye 2006; Hyde 2008; Schein 2018). These capacities, as discussed by Hart (2006), include wonder, wondering, relational spirituality, and wisdom. These capacities show up in the lives of young children as creativity, transcendence, awe, reverence, and love (Adams, Bull & Maynes 2016). They're also experienced by young children as inner peace and wonderment (Schein 2018), a sense of belonging (de Souza 2016), and meaning-making (Mata-McMahon, Haslip & Schein 2020).

In spite of research supporting the existence and manifestations of spirituality in children, a lack of clarity around this topic continues to impede greater awareness of its importance in the lives of young children. Unfortunately, this lack of clarity can also limit the amount of resources dedicated to enhancing the spiritual development of young children (Adams, Bull & Maynes 2016).

Spirituality and Play

Young children are naturally curious and eager to learn. Their approach to learning is based on play. They explore, create, question, experiment, and interact with others for the enjoyment of doing so. A young child will "gladly pluck weeds from paths or furrows, sweep up dried leaves or carry away an old branch" – not as work to be done but as playful activities inspired by an inner urge or "animating spirit prompting a child to make its way in the world" (Montessori 1986, p. 76).

Play, as the medium through which young children learn best, is self-chosen and self-directed, focused on the process instead of the product, individually constructed, imaginative and active. These and other characteristics of play are reflections of young children's spirituality. Maria Montessori (1986) – who referred to play as the work of the child – recognized play as having not only physical and cognitive dimensions but spiritual dimensions as well. The spiritual dimensions of play include joy and wonder, curiosity and creativity, transcendence, and a search for meaning. Understanding connections between creativity and spirituality reinforces the importance of play in the lives of young children.

Children make meaning of the world through play, and cooperative or collaborative play is especially powerful in the meaning-making process (Adams, Bull & Maynes 2016). Collaborative play, as a social activity, involves negotiating, problem-solving, and imagining together. Collaborative play often includes moments of care and compassion. These moments, along with other dimensions of play, combine not only to reflect the spiritual capacities of young children but to promote further spiritual development as well.

Montessori's emphasis on play is consistent with her views of the child as a spiritual being. She describes young children as having "unknown powers", "hidden possibilities", and an "absorbent mind." Montessori believed in a spiritual force, or embryo, that guides human development. She referred to the early years as being particularly crucial to the holistic and spiritual development of the child (Montessori 1972). Others, too, have identified the early years as crucial to the spiritual development of young children and have even suggested that spirituality may be the foundation, or drive, for all other areas of human development (Newberg & Newberg 2006; Schein 2018). Other historical figures in the field of education who recognized spirituality as an integral part of child development include Rudolf Steiner, founder of anthroposophy, and Friedrich Froebel (Fröbel), founder of the kindergarten.

BOX 2.1 IMPLICATIONS FOR PRACTICE: PLAYING WITH WORDS AND IDEAS

Young children's play often involves the use of materials. In constructive play, children use open-ended manipulative materials to make something. This type of play often includes a sense of purpose and planning. In dramatic play, children use something to stand for something else, like using a stick and pretending it's a magic wand. This type of play involves fantasy or make-believe. Another type of play involves playing with words and ideas instead of – or in addition to – materials. Sharing poetry with children is an excellent way to engage them in play with words and ideas. Each type of play, including sharing poetry with children, can be used to foster their spiritual development.

The aesthetics of poetic words and images help children appreciate beauty. The mystery often embedded in a poem fuels wonder and philosophical thinking. Nature-related poems can also promote deeper connections with the natural world.

"Who Has Seen the Wind?" by Christina Rossetti is an example of a poem with rich potential for reaping the many benefits of poetry for children. Sharing this poem with children can support them in becoming more aware and appreciative of everyday happenings in nature. It can also invite reflection on the wonders and mysteries of nature. Images of the tree's human-like actions of "trembling" and "bowing" can foster a sense of kinship with the trees.

Who Has Seen the Wind? By Christina Rossetti

Who has seen the wind?
Neither I nor you:
But when the leaves hang trembling,
The wind is passing through.

Who has seen the wind?
Neither you nor I:
But when the trees bow down their heads,
The wind is passing by.

> Interesting follow-up activities to the sharing of this poem could include inviting the children to "become the trees" as you read the poem. Children can also be invited to observe trees closely on a windy day, draw a picture of a tree as the wind blows through its branches and leaves, and watch what happens to other elements of nature on a windy day. For example, what happens to the water in a pond or to the fallen petals near the flower garden? (See Chapter 12 for a more detailed discussion about using nature-focused poetry to support young children's spirituality.)

Spirituality as a Basic Need

According to American psychologist Abraham Maslow, human actions are motivated by innate needs. One of our needs, he says, is to develop to our fullest potential or to achieve self-actualization. Self-actualizers, as described by Maslow (1954), live life with appreciation, joy, awe, and wonder. They may have mystical, self-transcendent experiences "characterized by intense ecstasy, bliss, and awe" (Ryff 2021, p. 3).

Maslow's theory of human motivation is referred to as a "hierarchy of needs" and is often depicted in the shape of a triangle or pyramid. Our most basic biological and physiological needs are at the bottom of the pyramid; our self-realization needs, at the top. From the bottom up, other levels of needs as outlined by Maslow are safety, social belonging, and self-esteem (Maslow 1954).

Another researcher, Nalini Nadkarni, proposed a revision of Maslow's hierarchy, highlighting the spiritual aspects of our growth-motivated needs. Her revisions reflect her extensive work in forest ecology. Nadkarni (2008) realized how nature – and trees, in particular – satisfy every level of need. Her revision includes seven levels of need. From the bottom of the pyramid to the apex, the levels are physical needs, security, health, play and imagination, time and history, symbols and language, spirituality, and mindfulness.

While Nadkarni's model is more explicit about spirituality being a basic human need, the concept is also embedded in Maslow's model. The spiritual aspects of Maslow's work haven't always been understood or appreciated. Some have even criticized his hierarchy of needs for what they interpret as a focus on self-absorption (Geller 1982). Critics of Maslow's hierarchy see the placement of "self-actualization" at the top of the hierarchy as a self-absorbed quest for personal fulfilment. This interpretation of Maslow's work fails to do justice to his theory. Maslow's later writings clarify what he meant by "self-actualization" – that it was never just about the self (Maslow 1971).

According to Maslow, self-actualization necessarily involves self-transcendence and other spiritual dimensions of the human experience of life on Earth. Self-transcendence includes moving beyond the self and having a concern for all of humanity. In other words, self-actualization as viewed by Maslow and others "contains an element of striving for the greater good" (Manjeera, Gundu & Rao 2024, p. 370).

Maslow's hierarchy suggests that our safety and survival goals need to be met before we can attend to goals at a higher level on the pyramid. Evidence indicates otherwise. "People readily demonstrate a willingness to sacrifice their safety and survival for the sake of something beyond themselves …. And this is regardless of age" (Gawande 2014, p. 93). Even young children demonstrate the ability and willingness to care deeply about something beyond themselves. In other words, young children can experience self-transcendence (Lithoxoidou et al. 2017; Weldemariam 2020).

Self-transcendence involves self-giving rather than self-absorption. It seeks to further a cause beyond one's own self-interests. "In other words, self-actualization cannot be attained if it is made an end in itself, but only as a side effect of self-transcendence" (Frankl 1959, p. 175).

Self-transcendence is also described as an experience that takes an individual beyond the boundaries of the self, through something called "peak experiences." Such experiences generally involve feelings of wonder and awe. They may also include a sense of timelessness. Peak experiences often occur in nature and may include "moments of fusion with nature" (Maslow 1962, p. 10).

The human need for spirituality isn't a need experienced by adults only. Research shows a clear, scientific link between spirituality and well-being in the lives of children (Coles 1990; Miller 2016). And, as noted earlier, spirituality may be the foundation for all other areas of child development (Schein 2018). This possibility is supported by research in the neuropsychology of spiritual experiences. Research by Andrew and Stephanie Newberg includes investigations into ways in which spirituality is linked with human biology and psychology throughout the life cycle. Their research supports the idea that spiritual experiences are linked to essential brain functions and optimal human development. Their research also indicates that spiritual experiences "can propel an individual along the developmental path" (Newberg & Newberg 2006, p. 184).

Conclusion

Spirituality is a basic human need, an essential element for quality of life, and an important contributor to a child's holistic development. Spirituality in the lives of young children is more than a momentary experience. Spirituality is a motivator, urging children to seek meaning, a sense of identity, and connections with the world around them.

Instinctual drives motivate every living being towards behaviours related to physical survival. Spirituality as a "coexistent source of motivation may be of a very different order" (Hart 2006, p. 174). Spirituality as a motivator includes a focus on interconnection, interdependence, and the drive to help others.

Spirituality, then, isn't just a frill or something nice to have. Nor should it appear in our work with young children as an afterthought or add-on. Giving children rich opportunities for engagement with nature is probably the best way to support their spirituality. Once nature is experienced as a "vale of soul-making," it can become a dependable strength that inhabits and shapes their lives over time.

While promoting the spiritual development of children offers numerous benefits to individual children, it can also make invaluable contributions to the nurturing of socially cohesive and caring communities. The importance of spirituality for children needs to be appreciated and nurtured in all the different dimensions of their lives, including their educational experiences.

We don't foster children's spirituality by trying to pour it in from the outside, for "children already have a spiritual life" (Hart 2006, p. 175). Our role in working with children is to respect their innate spiritual capacities and to provide the kind of physical and social environments that allow for the full expression of these capacities.

BOX 2.2   RESEARCH NOTE: TEACHER REFLECTIONS AND PRACTICES

Do efforts to support the holistic development of young children in public schools also promote spirituality? This question was used to frame a study conducted by researchers in the United States (Mata-McMahon, Haslip & Schein 2018, 2020). Because the U.S. Constitution calls for a separation between church and state, efforts to promote spirituality in public educational settings have generally been discouraged. This situation is based on the mistaken idea that religion and spirituality are synonymous. Do early childhood teachers see it this way?

Thirty-three early childhood educators working in secular settings in the U.S. completed surveys focusing on their perceptions and practices relating to young children's spirituality. Their responses indicated that they understood children's spirituality as relating to both the inner and outer life of the child and that it was more of a "heart strength" than a "mind strength." Their perceptions of children's spirituality included eight salient concepts: connections (including connections with nature), practicing virtues, making meaning, God and religion, self-awareness, mindfulness and presence, humanness, and inner feelings.

The teachers' responses also revealed a substantial overlap between developmentally appropriate practices and activities they used to support children's spirituality. Such practices included active engagement with nature (Mata-McMahon, Haslip & Schein 2018, 2020).

In an earlier study, Deborah Schein (2014) conducted in-depth interviews with twelve early childhood education specialists and reviewed journals kept by three of the study participants. One goal of this study was to identify nature's role in children's spiritual development. Results showed that children's spirituality, as perceived by the specialists, includes a sense of wonder and awe and that nature serves as a conduit for developing these attributes. Schein's later work (2018) included the publication of a book – *Inspiring Wonder, Awe, and Empathy* – offering guidance and thoughtful practices for promoting young children's spiritual development. One chapter is devoted entirely to nature engagement as a contributor to spiritual development.

3

Experiences in and with Nature

Tree Engagements

A preschooler and a teenager make discoveries as they strike wood on wood. The preschooler uses a stick to tap on trees as he walks through a forest. The teenager uses a bat to whack a tree as he walks home from baseball practice. The preschooler experiences what might be called an "aha moment." He shares his discovery with a teacher: "Every tree has a different song" (Warden 2011, p. 73).

The teenager – in writing about his tree experience – describes how whacking the tree was a senseless act. He didn't intend to hurt the tree, but a hard whack caused the young tree to break. The teenager watched as water trickled from the open wound. That's when he realized that the tree – like himself – had a circulatory system that kept it alive. This realization allowed him to experience kinship with the tree.

Environmental Epiphanies

What both the teenager and the preschooler discovered in their interactions with a tree might be described as an "environmental epiphany" – that is, a meaningful emotional experience with nature that provides a new insight into the human/nature connection (Vinning, Merrick & Price 2008). An environmental epiphany can leave a marked impression on an individual. It certainly did so for the teenager. Witnessing the tree "bleed", he said, shifted his relationship with trees. He gained a new appreciation of trees as living beings and knew that he would never whack a tree again.

Environmental epiphanies involve both the mind and the emotions and often lead to a shift in thinking and behaviour. Such shifts can play an important role in shaping pro-environmental attitudes and behaviours. A "facts-only approach" that has sometimes been used in environmental education programs has generally proven to be ineffective in promoting pro-environmental attitudes and behaviours (Lumber, Richardson & Sheffield 2017). An embodied pedagogy that involves the senses and emotions and physicality tends to be more effective in meeting the goals of environmental education (Wills 2025).

At one time, emotions were considered to be disruptive to rational decision-making. More recent and research-backed understandings, however, indicate that emotions are highly influential and valuable to learning and to the decision-making process (Isen 2000).

Interacting with Nature

A child using a stick to tap on trees isn't unusual. Peter Kahn, a researcher at the University of Washington, identified "striking wood on wood" as a typical "interaction pattern" for young children (Kahn, Weiss & Harrington 2018). Other nature-related interaction patterns identified by Kahn and colleagues include hanging from tree limbs, climbing high in small trees, lying on earth, constructing shelter, and digging in ground. These interactions with nature typically occur without any prompting from adults. They "have been part of our evolution as a species and/or are important today for an individual's development and well-being" (Gray et al. 2025, p. 2).

The child who discovered that "every tree has a different song" was participating in a Forest School program, where the children with their teachers spend the entire school day in a forest setting. Such a setting allows the children to make many magical discoveries. The importance of magical moments in nature as part of the learning process should not be underestimated. Learning involves far more than absorbing facts. The most meaningful and joyful learning involves discovery, sometimes in the form of "ta-da" moments. Such moments tend to stimulate growth and transformation. They can shift not only our way of thinking about but also our way of relating to the world around us.

As the child used a stick to tap on different trees in the forest, he noticed that different trees produced different sounds. From this experience, the child learned that not all trees are the same, that there must be something inside the trees that made them different. This was something new the child learned through his own explorations and observations. It was an exciting discovery.

The way this child learned something new about the natural world is a distinctive feature of Forest School. A Forest School curriculum is basically an emergent – rather than pre-set – curriculum. Teachers using an emergent curriculum plan activities, materials, and projects based on the specific interests and characteristics of the group of children they are working with. An emergent curriculum also considers the concerns, abilities, and interests of each individual child. This approach is child-centred and reflects an understanding and appreciation of the way that young children learn and develop. This approach, when used in Forest School, provides rich opportunities for children to establish and enjoy an on-going relationship with the land and to make many exciting discoveries about the natural world and about themselves.

Unfortunately, for the majority of children today, time is spent in built environments, which tend to be regulated and often static. Most of these places are designed by and for adults. Natural environments are different. Natural environments offer a type of sensory richness not experienced in most built environments. Elements of a natural environment are varied and changing. Many children enjoy the fact that the forest and other natural environments are, for them, "strange and unfamiliar, surprising and unplanned" (Schirp & Vollmar 2013, p. 32).

It's also unfortunate that much of what children are expected to learn are pre-packaged facts and understandings. In traditional educational settings, that's what they are tested on as indicators of academic success.

What Nature Offers

Play is critical to a young child's holistic development, and most children are good at finding a way to play in almost any environment. The type and quality of their play, however, are influenced by the physical, social, and cultural features of the environment.

Many communities have designated areas for children to play. These areas – often referred to as "playgrounds" or "playspaces" – show up in all kinds of settings: schools, parks, shopping malls, and even airports. Some of the playgrounds are entirely devoid of "ground" and offer limited opportunities for various types of play. Thus, they're not really "playgrounds." A forest as a playspace is entirely different. While a forest may not be called a playground, the play opportunities it offers are rich and endless. In fact, most natural environments offer more affordances for play than traditional playgrounds (Wishart et al. 2019). (See Chapter 8 for more information about the play affordances of natural environments and the benefits of nature play for children.)

Affordances allow organisms to interact with their habitats in active and purposeful ways. James Gibson (1979) introduced the term in reference to how animals interact with their environments: "The affordances of the environment are what it offers the animal, what it provides or furnishes, either for good or ill" (p. 119). Gibson's description of affordances, however, refers to more than the physical properties of what's in the environment. The concept of affordances implies a "complementarity of the animal and the environment" (p. 119).

Affordances have been described in the academic literature as "meaningful action possibilities" (Lerstrup, Chawla & Heft 2021, p. 58). Affordances work like invitations – they invite children to explore and experiment in playful ways. Some affordances are "loose parts" that children can manipulate as they explore and experiment. Natural materials, such as stones and sticks, are loose parts; so are such manufactured materials as digging tools and sprinkling cans. An affordance can also be something "fixed in place", like a tree, a climbing wall, and a table or a shelf. Affordances can be people as well.

There's more to affordances than what the materials, fixtures, or people in the environment have to offer. Functional significance or functional meaning also plays a role. "The affordances of the environment are its functionally significant properties considered in relation to an individual" (Heft 1988, p. 29). Gibson (1979) describes this relationship by saying that an affordance "is equally a fact of the environment and a fact of behavior. ... An affordance points both ways, to the environment and to the observer" (p. 120). Thus, referencing a tree as an affordance for climbing is applicable only to a child who has the ability to climb. This aspect of affordances becomes especially important in working with children of different ages, interests, and abilities.

One reason why a natural environment is so conducive to learning and child development relates to the varied and rich affordances in that environment. Affordances are often viewed in relation to inanimate entities and the opportunities they provide for physical activities, such as running, building, and climbing. Affordances, however, can include small animals, which offer invitations for observations and interactions.

A related study, which included multiple observations of children in a forest setting, found that children are fascinated by small animals (such as insects, worms, snails, and frogs) and readily become engaged with them in hands-on activities. These activities included searching for wild creatures, catching and releasing them, and acting out such animal behaviours as building nests and digging in the ground. Staff members described how the children "treated creatures like treasures, and each interaction appeared to ignite wonder and awe" (Lerstrup, Chawla & Heft 2021, p. 66). Teachers also noted how experiences with a variety of creatures promoted deep and positive relations between the children, the creatures, and their habitats.

Another study focusing on children in a forest setting asked teachers and children to share ideas about what they liked best in the forest (Lerstrup & Refshauge 2016). A variety of forest features were mentioned, but "loose objects" (or "loose parts") were mentioned most frequently. Loose objects included such natural materials as plant parts (sticks, leaves, seeds, etc.), soil, water, and stones. This same study included observations of children during free play in the forest. Data from the observations indicated that children found small creatures and "animal leftovers" (bones, feathers, fur, etc.) especially intriguing. Children were also attracted to such special features as "a slanting stump, a forked tree, a branch for swinging, or closely growing trees that allowed children to climb from one to the other" (Lerstrup & Refshauge 2016, p. 394). Crooked sticks and strange stones also caught the children's interest, as did such new and different features as water turning to ice and a tree felled by a storm.

Natural areas and natural materials also offer invitations and possibilities for deeply spiritual experiences. An environmental epiphany is just one type of spiritual experience children might have in nature. There are others, including transcendent experiences, aesthetic experiences, and connectedness experiences.

Transcendent Experiences

A transcendent experience reflects the intrapersonal (within the child) dimension of spiritual development. This dimension shows up in the child as mindfulness, curiosity, imagination, self-awareness, wonder, wonderment, joy, awe, and inner peace. One attribute of the child which makes the unfolding of the intrapersonal dimension of spirituality possible is the "absorbent mind", which was recognized by Montessori (1972) as an inherent quality of the young child.

Deborah Schein (2018) describes the absorbent mind as the "mental, social, and emotional capacity to engage and connect to the outside world" (p. 20). Clearly evident in this description is the understanding that the absorbent mind relates to more than what is processed in the brain. The workings and impact of the absorbent mind are much broader than that. The absorbent mind helps to shape self-awareness, which is more than the mental construct of who we are as individuals. The absorbent mind opens the way for connections with the world outside of oneself (Schein 2018).

Once these connections are in place, the child is in a position to move beyond – or transcend – the boundaries of self. Transcendence, in this sense, shifts attention away from the self to something greater or more awesome than self. This form of transcendence often includes a sense of oneness and feelings of awe.

The experience of awe may be accompanied by – or initiated by – astonishment, surprise, and amazement. We may experience awe when encountering something vaster or greater than or beyond our current understanding (Keltner & Haidt 2003). At times, we may experience awe as we witness exceptional generosity, courage, or skill performance of other people. Awe can also be felt in such non-social situations as hiking alone in the mountains or contemplating works of art. Noticing the amazing abundance of such elements in nature as the number of leaves on a tree or the stars in the sky can also generate awe and feelings of transcendence. Young children may experience awe in response to what adults may consider ordinary happenings of daily life, such as the splashing of a bird in a birdbath or the movement of a butterfly from one blossom to another.

Awe experiences – which tend to occur more often in nature than other settings (Shiota, Keltner & Mossman 2007) – come with physical, emotional, and spiritual benefits for both adults and children. One study found that the well-being benefits of awe include the engagement of five processes: positive shifts in neurophysiology, a diminished focus on the self, increased prosocial relationality, greater social integration, and a heightened sense of meaning (Monroy & Keltner 2023). A review of the literature focusing specifically on the benefits of awe-inspiring encounters with nature found additional benefits for children, including an increase in social connections, perspective taking, and prosocial behaviours (Goldy & Piff 2020).

Aesthetic Experiences

Aesthetics generally means an appreciation of beauty, with appreciation being linked to what is both recognized and enjoyed. We might thus assume that an aesthetic experience is based on what we cognitively perceive and emotionally feel. An aesthetic experience for the young child, however, may be broader and more holistic than that. It may involve the entire body, mind, and spirit.

Children are less likely than adults to divide the world – and their experience of the world – into categories established through human cognition. Whereas an adult may view "getting caught in the rain" as an unpleasant bodily experience, a child may view this same experience in a qualitatively different way. To young children, walking in the rain may be a very aesthetic experience. As adults, we usually consider rain – or, more generally, the weather – to be something external to ourselves. We might make contact with the weather and may feel its impact on our bodies yet think of the weather as something separate from ourselves.

Unless taught otherwise, young children may experience the weather differently. A child may experience the different sensory dimensions not only *of rain* (wetness, sound, smell, etc.) but also *of oneself in the rain*. This consciousness of the body experience can strengthen the aesthetic and spiritual dimensions of the body/nature encounter. (See Chapter 11 for additional ideas about helping children know and appreciate weather as something more than a backdrop or context for human activities.)

BOX 3.1   REFLECTIONS: LEARNING IN AND WITH THE WEATHER

Weather-related activities, projects, and books are often included in typical early childhood education curricula. The focus of related "lessons" is usually on *learning about the weather* as something separate from humans. Tonya Rooney (2018) proposes a different approach. She suggests tapping into children's lively curiosity by offering "more situated and entangled ways of learning in and 'with' weather."

Doing so, she says, "may open up alternative, less human-centric ways of coming to know and respond to the environmental challenges ahead" (p. 1).

Rooney's ideas about "learning in and with weather" are based on a concept called "common worlding" or "commons world." This concept recognizes humans as beings in common (or co-habiting) with other species and elements of the natural world (Pacini-Ketchabaw, Taylor & Blaise 2016). A story told by Rooney (2018) illustrates how a young child notices and experiments with her own self as being part of the weather world. She refers to this as "weather worlding." The child notices "little clouds of air" drifting near her as she breathes while outside on a very cold day. Once noticing the way visible condensation forms as her warm breath moves through the cold air, the child breathes more deliberately and forcibly to continue making "little clouds" that follow her.

Rooney discusses the significance of "weather worlding" by connecting it to concerns about climate change. She describes how a "weather worlding" approach to environmental education attends more directly to child/weather relations and opens up "possible ways of responding to climate change that shift the focus beyond human-centric concerns" (Rooney 2018, p. 8). One of the practical suggestions Rooney offers on how to use a "weather worlding" approach with young children involves "walking in the weather" or – as she also says – "walking with the weather." The simple practice of "walking with the weather may offer a starting point for understanding our inter-connectedness with the weather world" (p. 9).

Aesthetic experiences generally bring us joy, giving us an emotional uplift. Aesthetic experiences – especially when they involve awe – tend to shift our focus away from self and from our individual worries or concerns. We may feel "wrapped up" in the wonder of the moment. That "wrapped up" feeling is what a child may experience when "getting caught in the rain" and when deeply immersed in other nature-related experiences.

Connectedness Experiences

As noted earlier, awe experiences in nature can foster enhanced social connections, perspective taking, sensitivity to others, and prosocial behaviours (Goldy & Piff 2020). These positive outcomes of experiences in nature are examples of what Tobin Hart (2006) refers to as "relational spirituality," an interpersonal dimension of children's spiritual development.

Relational spirituality manifests in children through connectedness with other people but also through "a profound sense of interconnection with the cosmos" (Hart 2006, p. 174). Just as early childhood is a unique time when children are forming meaningful relationships with other people in their lives, it is also a critically important time for children to be exploring their relationship with the more-than-human world (Beery, Chawla & Levin 2020). Exploring this relationship – or becoming aware of self in relation to the environment – is something young children have demonstrated they are capable of doing (Konerman et al. 2021; McClain & Vandermaas-Peeler 2016). Young children are also capable of developing caring attitudes about the more-than-human world. This was demonstrated by one young child deciding not to pick some flowers due to a concern about possibly hurting them (McClain & Vandermaas-Peeler, 2016) and a group of preschoolers showing concern for dying bees on the playground (Nxumalo 2017; Weldermariam and Wals 2020).

BOX 3.2   RESEARCH NOTE: CO-HABITING VS. DOMINATION

A study of young children in Hong Kong compared how children interacted with nature in two different environments: one a relatively wild (unmanaged) natural area and the other a more domesticated (managed) natural area (Lam, Kahn & Weiss 2023). The coding of children's self-directed play behaviours differentiated between domination interaction patterns and relational interaction patterns. Domination interaction behaviours included aggression toward nature, attempts to control nature, and actions causing harm to nature. Relational interaction behaviours, on the other hand, reflected a positive bond with nature or a respectful awareness of nature.

Results showed that children in the domesticated nature area engaged in more domination interaction patterns (e.g., catching wild animals) but that children in the unmanaged nature areas engaged in more relational interaction patterns (e.g., cohabitating with wild animals). These findings suggest that one way to shift human consciousness away from a domination worldview and toward relational living is to give children more opportunities to interact with relatively wild nature.

Reference

Lam, L-W., Kahn Jr, P.H. & Weiss, T. (2023). Children in Hong Kong interacting with relatively wild nature (vs. domestic nature) engage in less dominating and more relational behaviours. *Environmental Education Research*, 29(9), 1294–1309.

Connectedness to Nature Domains

"Connectedness to nature" is generally described as having three domains: cognitive, emotional, and experiential/behavioural. These domains correspond to "how we think, feel, and act about/in the natural world" (Barrable, Friedman & Beloyianni 2024).

The cognitive domain consists of the mental representations or perceptions (mindset) held by an individual regarding their relationship with nature. This domain is sometimes described as the extent to which individuals perceive nature as part of their identity (Barrable, Friedman & Beloyianni 2024; Schultz 2002). The emotional domain consists of feelings of belonging or closeness with nature (Barrable, Friedman & Beloyianni 2024; Mayer & Frantz 2004). This domain includes an individual's sense of care for nature (Schultz 2002). The experiential/behavioural domain includes time spent in nature and an individual's actions to protect the natural environment (Schultz 2002).

A closer look at each of these domains reveals a spiritual dimension. Cognitively, one's mental representations may include an awareness of unity and oneness; emotionally, one may experience feelings of transcendence; and behaviourally, one may be inspired to act beyond self-interests. Each of these experiences or responses is a manifestation of spirituality. Other manifestations of the spiritual dimensions of connectedness to nature include awareness and enjoyment of nature, feelings of wonder, empathy, responsibility, and curiosity (Adams, Bull & Maynes 2016; Giesenberg 2000; Hart 2006; Schein 2018).

What children experience while physically, cognitively, and sensually engaged with the natural environment can lead to the experience of spiritual moments (de Souza 2016; Hay & Nye 2006; Schein 2018). Schein (2018) discusses five types of spiritual moments that young children might experience: (1) in time (often reflecting mindfulness), (2) in space (often involving aesthetics or beauty), (3) in and with nature (through wonderment, awe, joy, and inner peace), (4) in strong relationships (as manifested in empathy, respect, and kindness), and (5) with big questions (reflecting radical amazement and going beyond oneself).

In addition to sustained contact with nature, key factors in setting the stage for spiritual moments in nature include focusing on nature's beauty, cultivating compassion towards non-human nature, and practicing mindfulness (Barrable 2019). Also important is uninterrupted time in nature (Hattingh 2024) with opportunities for reflection or introspection (Cree & Robb 2021).

Conclusion

The spiritual dimensions of connectedness to nature touch both the inner and outer life of the child. Curiosity leads young children to closely observe and physically interact with the elements of nature. What they experience and discover through such interactions often engender feelings of wonder, awe, and reverence for the natural world. What children experience and discover through such interactions can also lead to "the having of wonderful ideas" (Duckworth 2006) which can greatly benefit the children and the world in which we live.

BOX 3.3 IMPLICATIONS FOR PRACTICE: PLAYFUL EXPERIENCES IN THE FOREST

Observations of children in different environments indicate that they engage in more complex and creative forms of play in outdoor natural environments than in traditional playgrounds or indoors (Luchs & Fikus 2013; Morrissey, Scott & Rahimi 2017; Storli & Sandseter 2019; Zamani 2016). With this in mind, just imagine the play opportunities of children in a forest! The children can build forts and stone structures, climb trees and crawl over logs, collect leaves and pinecones, search for critters, make exciting discoveries (jaw bones!), and dance with the wind. While the loose parts of the forest environment provide almost endless opportunities for hands-on manipulation, the mystery of the forest also engages the imagination of young children and invites the manipulation of ideas. Children readily become other-than-human creatures with all kinds of magical powers. They may see fairies in the trees and hear voices in a cave or stream.

Of course, not all children have regular access to a forest, but they can and should have daily access to a natural environment and natural materials where they can engage in all types of creative play. If you don't have access to a forest, you can increase children's play opportunities by taking advantage of such natural areas as a ditch bank, an urban park or nature preserve, or even the shaded area around a single tree. For both indoor and outdoor playspaces, you can also provide a rich variety of natural materials for children to manipulate: sand, water, soil, stones, shells, seeds, leaves, and so on. And, if you have a more traditional playground, do what you can to transform it into a more natural environment. Add a garden, a bird bath, a digging area. Plant berry bushes and watermelon vines. You might even use forest floor materials to cover part of the playspace.

One childcare centre in Finland added a forest floor with high biodiversity, sod, peat blocks, and planters for growing vegetables and flowers. A survey completed by 13 employees of the centre one month after the natural materials were added to the yard noted how these materials provided multi-sensory experiences for the children and how the children engaged in more diverse play and nature exploration (Puhakka et al. 2019).

An excellent resource for more information and ideas relating to green schoolyards and the benefits they have to offer is the Children & Nature Network website (https://www.childrenandnature.org/schools/).

4

Spiritual Benefits

The Nature/Spirituality Connection

Nature as a pathway to spirituality isn't a new idea. As journalist Richard Louv (2006), notes, "Most people are either awakened to or are strengthened in their spiritual journey by experiences in the natural world" (p. 296). A number of research studies supports this idea (Dutcher et al. 2007; Hedlund-de Witt 2013; Williams & Harvey 2001). One such study found that "there frequently appears to be a spiritual dimension to profound experiences in the natural world" (Hedlund-de Witt 2013, p. 156). This particular study involved two groups of people: environmentalists and adults in spirituality groups. People in the environmentalist group appeared to be committed to spiritual practices and beliefs almost as much as people in the spirituality groups. People in the spirituality groups, on the other hand, often expressed almost as much love and reverence for nature as the environmentalists did.

Individuals in both groups indicated that their relationships with nature started early in life and that their experiences included participating in and communing with nature. They "spoke about nature in an explicitly relational and reciprocal way, describing nature as friend, guide, or companion, who helped them to resolve problems, get inspiration, and wisdom, or ease loneliness" (Hedlund-de Witt 2013, p. 165).

An interesting aspect of this research relates to how profound experiences with nature often lead to spirituality, while spirituality often leads to a deeper connectedness with nature. In other words, engagement with nature and attention to spirituality tend to reinforce each other. An impressive body of research supports these mutually reinforcing aspects of nature connectedness and spirituality (Crawford & Holder 2012; Frederickson & Anderson 1999; Kaplan & Talbot 1983; Keltner & Haidt 2003; Williams & Harvey 2001). One review identified over 300 articles relating to nature connectedness and spirituality. This review highlighted ways in which connectedness with nature "supports happiness and more purposeful, fulfilling, and meaningful lives" (Zylstra et al. 2014, p. 119). An August 2024 search of the Children & Nature Network (C&NN) Research Library identified 50 articles reporting spiritual outcomes as a benefit of children's engagement with nature. These spiritual outcomes include mindfulness, caring and concern for other living things, transcendence, and creativity.

BOX 4.1   REFLECTIONS: A SPIRITUAL MOMENT

One of my chores growing up on a farm was to water the chickens. I had to do this every day to keep the chickens healthy. The chickens were an important resource for our family. They were a source of income and food. I must have been about seven years old when something shifted in my relationship with the chickens.

It was early evening when it started to storm. I remember strong wind, thunder, and rain. My Dad put on a raincoat and invited me to go with him to check on the baby chicks that had been delivered to the farm earlier in the day. He was concerned about the sound of the storm possibly frightening the chicks and causing them to crowd together. This could suffocate them.

We walked through the rain to the chicken coop, carrying a lantern and a radio with us. We were hoping that the radio would muffle the sound of the storm. Once inside the chicken coop, I sat on the floor and held a baby chick in my hand. I immediately noticed how soft and small it was. The chick was chirping loudly and seemed anxious and frightened. I could feel its heart beating. That's when I realized that the chick was more than a resource, that the chick and I had something in common. We were both living beings with beating hearts. The chick, like me, could experience fear and uncertainty.

Fortunately, the chicks survived the storm, and I continued to water them every day. Doing so, however, was different. I viewed the chickens in a different light. They were no longer just a resource. They were kin.

Feeling the heartbeat of the baby chick was a spiritual moment for me. Holding the baby chick and sensing its fear and vulnerability took me outside of myself. My concern for its welfare went far beyond what we would lose if the chicks died. I cared about the chick as another living being with its own sensibilities.

After that evening, watering the chickens was no longer just a chore for me. I knew I was taking care of other living beings. I started to really notice the chickens as I brought water to them each day. At times, I even talked to them.

Nature for Healing

People of all ages, with differing abilities, and from different backgrounds often discover that nature can be a source of healing and a place of peace. This was certainly true for Eve, now an adult, who faced challenges related to a sight impairment ever since she was a child. Her "salvation" was to spend time in nature. This is where she could be comfortable on her own terms. According to Eve, "This is where I feel most at peace, most secure, most stress free" (Bell 2019, p. 313). Other people with special needs have expressed similar experiences. They look to nature for acceptance and a sense of belonging. It's in nature that they find "moments of peace" (Bell 2019, p. 308). For Eve, such moments are often lacking while engaged with other people.

Abbie, another adult with sight impairment, also experiences discomfort around other people. She attributes this to attitudes that people sometimes have about individuals with disabilities. Such attitudes, she notes, tend to discourage rather than encourage a sense of independence (Bell 2019). Nature doesn't do that. Nature doesn't judge or discriminate.

Tiffany, an adult who works with young children with special needs in a forest preschool, explains how children experience a sense of calm while in the forest and how what they observe is comforting. "As they visit the same places over time, children see that the leaves are still growing on the trees, the water in the creek is still flowing, and the ants are still moving about" (Wilson 2022, p. 16). Rachel Carson, scientist and author, said something similar: "There is something infinitely healing in the repeated refrains of nature – the assurance that dawn comes after night, and spring after winter" (Carson 1956, pp. 88–89).

Christine, a teacher educator working with nature-based programs, finds nature to be a calming element for both teachers and children. She says, "One of the secret ingredients in outdoor learning may be in how nature supports feelings of calm and tranquility" (Wilson 2022, p. 67). The healing powers of nature have been noted by many others as well. Documented benefits to children and youth include (1) adolescents with complex trauma issues finding healing through outdoor adventure (Pringle et al. 2023), (2) nature therapy providing both restorative and preventative benefits for children experiencing adversity (Fisher 2022), (3) forest healing programs proving helpful to children in foster care (Hong, Park & An 2021), (4) healing gardens helping youth with autism meet their therapeutic goals (Scartazza et al. 2020), and (5) natural elements added to paediatric healthcare settings promoting the health and well-being of children who are ill (Gaminiesfahani, Lozanovska & Tucker 2020).

Related research also indicates that nature can reduce the negative impact of potentially traumatic events experienced by children during their early childhood years. In other words, nature may serve as a "buffer" (or protective factor) for children before the harmful impacts of adverse childhood experiences on development occur (Touloumakos & Barrable 2020). Positive nature experiences could also be helpful to children suffering from climate change anxiety and other nature-related concerns (Buchanan, Pressick-Kilborn & Fergusson 2021; Thoma, Rohleder & Rohner 2021; Sanson, Van Hoorn & Burke 2019).

> **BOX 4.2   RESEARCH NOTE: AWE IN NATURE HEALS**
>
> Researchers conducted two separate studies to test the idea that nature promotes well-being through awe. This research was based on previous studies showing that contact with nature can reduce stress and enhance well-being. It was also based on research documenting the power of nature to elicit awe. This follow-up research combined these two previous lines of inquiry by examining the role of awe in the process of healing through contact with nature.
>
> Study 1 focused on awe as experienced during white-water rafting. Seventy-two military veterans and 52 youth (middle and high school students) representing a wide range of racial/cultural backgrounds and life experiences participated in either a one-day or a four-day whitewater rafting trip. All participants were from underserved communities.
>
> At the end of each rafting day, participants completed a rafting diary noting the extent to which they experienced six different positive emotions (awe, gratitude, amusement, pride, contentment, and joy) during the day. Measures of well-being were also completed before and after the rafting trips. Assessment results indicated that experiences of awe during the rafting trip had a greater positive impact on well-being than the other assessed emotions (amusement, contentment, gratitude, joy, and pride).
>
> Study 2 in this research extended the findings of Study 1 by examining the link between nature experience, awe, and well-being in the context of people's everyday lives. Over 100 undergraduate students participated in this study. Every night, over a period of 14 consecutive days, participants completed a diary survey delivered by e-mail.

The survey included questions focusing on emotions, social experiences, and thoughts that participants experienced during the day. The survey included an open-ended section in which participants were asked to write about an experience of awe they had that day or about the most positive event of the day. Participants also completed well-being assessments before and after the 14-day diary period.

Findings of this study showed that more nature experiences were linked to greater daily life satisfaction and greater improvements in well-being. Findings also showed that "awe, above and beyond the effects of other positive emotions," was linked to daily life satisfaction. This research didn't focus on young children but is mentioned in this book to highlight the impact of awe experiences on human well-being. One of the gifts of nature relates to awe which enriches the lives of people of all ages.

Reference

Anderson, C. L., Monroy, M. & Keltner, D. (2018). Awe in nature heals: Evidence from military veterans, at-risk youth, and college students. *Emotion*, *18*(8), 1195–1202.

Nature for Transcendence

As noted earlier, one of the spiritual benefits of nature is the experience of transcendence or transcending oneself. This experience generally includes the realization that we are part of something greater than ourselves. Awe-inspiring encounters with nature, which often engender feelings of transcendence, can increase tendencies to care for, help, and assist others, with the "others" including the more-than-human world (Goldy & Piff 2020).

One of the questions addressed in the literature relates to the long-term benefits of nature-related experiences. A 2022 study by researchers in Australia addressed this question. The specific aim of the study was to better understand how a singular, meaningful experience in nature might shape an individual's relationship with nature, change their social relationships, and influence environmental decisions and behaviours (Mathers & Brymer 2022). The researchers interviewed 21 adults who had experienced a profound experience with nature. During the interviews, participants were asked to describe their profound experience and the impact it had on their lives.

All of the interviewees identified ways in which the experience had changed their lives. For some, the changes were primarily nature-related, such as being more mindful of resource use and spending more time in natural settings. One woman described how a profound experience in nature inspired her to travel to a remote part of India to learn about the relationship between spirituality and the forest. Several of the participants recounted how their profound experience helped them gain a better understanding of themselves and how to become more aligned with their core values and beliefs. For some, the experience expanded their spiritual beliefs. One participant said that she felt supported, safe, and loved. All of the participants expressed the importance of their profound experience with nature in their life and acknowledged its positive long-term effects.

While this study was conducted with adults, the personal story shared in Box 4.1 ("A Spiritual Moment") illustrates how a profound experience with nature can provide deeply spiritual insights. Studies with children have shown similar results (Adams & Beauchamp 2021; Adams & Beauchamp 2019).

Benefits for Families and the Larger Community

While child engagement with nature benefits both the child and the environment, it also benefits families, communities, and the larger society. One mother, in noting how time in nature benefits the entire family, described it as a "shared joy and a shared communion with nature" (Wilson 2022, p. 72). Related research shows that the benefits of shared nature-related experiences for families include reduced stress (Izenstark, Crossman & Middaugh 2021; Izenstark & Ebata 2019), close interaction (Rantala & Puhakka 2020), and enhanced emotional connection and communication (Mattsson et al. 2022). One study with Latinx families found that shared experiences in nature reaffirmed their sense of connectedness to family and culture (Izenstark, Crossman & Middaugh 2021).

Another study found that outdoor play spaces "are not only places where children play, but also where family life and childhood are 'built'" (Chen, Yuan & Zhu 2019, p. 1). An interesting aspect of one study focusing on the benefits of family camping includes a discussion about the spiritual aspects of the experience (Jirásek, Roberson & Jirásková 2017). Some of the adults in this study felt a "spiritual dynamic" in the community of families coming together. One adult described this dynamic as "transcendence with mutual enrichment" (p. 87).

Understandings about the multiple benefits of nature for families have led to the development of health-care initiatives encouraging families to spend more time outdoors in natural settings. One such initiative involves "park prescriptions", which include general advising and/or written prescriptions for families to spend time together in a park or other natural area. Related research includes a study aimed at determining if park prescriptions would improve stress and other behavioural and health outcomes for parents at a low-income clinic. Assessments conducted at various times throughout the study showed an increase in park visits per week and a significant and incremental decrease in stress. Other positive outcomes of the park prescription program included increases in physical activity and nature affinity and decreases in loneliness and physiological stress (Razani et al. 2018).

Communities around the world are discovering that investments in nature yield benefits for the community. In some places, community investments in nature take the form of green schoolyards and nature-smart libraries. Other initiatives include increasing the quality and quantity of greenspace open to the public, establishing community gardens, encouraging urban agriculture, expanding urban forestry, and cleaning up waterways and vacant lots.

The greening of schoolyards – especially in urban communities – provides a clear example of how children, communities, and the environment benefit from an investment in nature. With schoolyard greening, more traditional schoolyards are renovated to become nature-rich environments, which may include native gardens, nature play areas, vegetable gardens, trails, trees, and water features. The primary goal, in many cases, relates to enhancing children's play and learning opportunities. But other goals can be addressed as well. Schoolyard greening can help cities meet some of their green infrastructure goals, such as stormwater management and urban heat island reduction.

Schoolyard greening can also be used to advance equitable access to nature, which may help reduce disparities in multiple dimensions of quality of life. There's no doubt that children and families living in less-advantaged neighbourhoods are generally at greater risk for poor outcomes in the areas of physical health and mental health, social and educational outcomes, and overall well-being. Research indicates that increased access to nature may benefit individuals in less-advantaged situations more than those with greater economic advantage (Alderton et al. 2019). This effect is referred to as equigenesis or the equigenic effect.

The equigenic effect basically disrupts the usual relationship between economic disadvantage and poor quality-of-life outcomes. It, in effect, makes lower and higher economic status groups more equal. The benefits of equigenesis apply to individuals, groups, and the larger community.

One of the major initiatives of the C&NN focuses on the development of green schoolyards. More information about this initiative and related research documenting the multiple benefits of green schoolyards can be found at the C&NN website (https://www.childrenandnature.org/). Green Schools America (https://www.greenschoolyards.org/) and Learning Through Landscapes (https://ltl.org.uk/) also offer a wealth of related information.

BOX 4.3 SUGGESTIONS: "GO GREEN" WITH PEACE EDUCATION

An article published in *Exchange* magazine in 2009 proposed making the colour green a "go" for peace education (Wilson 2009). The article was based on the understanding that fostering a sense of caring, respect, and empathy for plants and animals would address the goals of both environmental education and peace education. It would also support the spiritual development of the child.

"Going green" with peace education was discussed as a way to enhance the soulfulness of early childhood education. It was also discussed in relation to education for social responsibility with a focus on the development of "humans as nurturers cooperating to preserve the natural world and human communities" (Mische & Harris 2008).

Several suggestions were offered for applying the "green approach" to peace education at the early childhood level. Here are a few of these suggestions:

- Model and validate caring behaviours. You might do this by taking care not to step on fragile plants while walking through a natural area or by sharing produce from your garden with children from another classroom and/or with people in the community.
- Identify and share children's literature that carry messages about living in harmony with other people and the rest of the natural world. *Home in the Sky* by Jeannie Baker and *If You Were My Baby* by Fran Hodgkins and Laura Bryant are examples of children's books with peace-related messages.
- Provide opportunities for children to assist in the care of simple things in nature. One example is to give children active roles in maintaining a bird bath, especially during hot and dry times of the year.

> "Going green" with peace education is offered as a way to help children develop a sense of themselves as nurturing and caring people. This sense of self can contribute to a peaceful way of living – with self, with other people, and with the rest of the natural world.

Conclusion

Attending to the spiritual dimensions of humans' affinity for nature can benefit children, families, communities, and the natural environment. For children, the spiritual benefits of nature engagement include increased mindfulness, caring and concern for other living things, transcendence, and creativity. These benefits are too profound and long-lasting to be dismissed or ignored.

5

Spiritual Roots

Savouring and Saving

Trees – as diverse as they are – share certain characteristics. They all have roots and branches. In some ways, humans and human institutions are like trees. We, as humans, have a trunk and limbs. We stand upright, come in different sizes, and have a circulatory system that plays an important role in keeping us alive. The institutions that we create – such as schools, churches, legal systems, and special interest groups – have roots and branches. Their roots – which hold them in place – include the beliefs and aims on which they were founded. The branches of an institution reflect ways in which they reach out into society.

I once asked Sally Stevens, the founder and director of SOL [Soulful Outdoor Learning] Forest School in New Mexico, if the focus of her work with children is more on savouring or saving the natural world. Her answer in a return email was clear:

> It's definitely more about 'savoring' vs 'saving'. In fact, I rarely (if ever) use the phrase 'saving the earth/nature' as this is just too much to put upon our little Treeschoolers & I KNOW that in the slowing down, noticing, & being in our bodies, which is essentially 'savoring' the Natural

World, the 'saving' does & will occur in the form of future stewards.

(Stevens 2024)

As Sally's response indicates, savoring nature does more than provide a momentary "feel good" experience. It nourishes and enlarges the heart and soul of the child. It ignites wonder, joy, and excitement. While savoring nature is experienced with the body, it's felt with the soul. Savoring nature can lead to increased creativity, curiosity, and caring. And, as Sally and others have indicated, savoring nature leads to saving nature.

I presented a similar question to Juliet Stavely, an early childhood educator who works with the Railyard Conservancy in Santa Fe, New Mexico. Juliet's response included the following:

> I see it as considering both [savoring and saving], looking at each through different lens, that then share a lens.... children have it in them to be curious about nature at a young age, they savor it, they have the biophilia, the innate connection.... In early childhood education, it is so much about the savoring of the connections with nature, and creating those spaces, experiences to do it in. They [children] are the next generation of nature stewards and they will need those early memories as a reference, to carry with them as they tackle with hardships from climate change and advocate for saving.
>
> (Stavely 2024)

Both Sally's and Juliet's responses are consistent with what researchers and many other practitioners are discovering. Young children's engagement with nature often involves both savoring and saving nature (Hoover 2021). Without prompting from adults, young children seem drawn to the sounds, textures, smells, colours, and movements of nature. They often respond with laughter or joy, intense concentration, and wonder (Wilson 2018). Yet savoring nature isn't at the expense of saving nature. In fact, savoring nature can lead to efforts to save nature (Chawla 2009; van Heel, van den Born & Aarts 2023; Wills 2025).

Both savoring and saving experiences often show up in young children's nature play activities. Individual studies, as well as a review of research, indicate that nature play can promote dispositions and skills relevant to sustainability (Ernst & Burcak 2019; Ernst et al. 2021). In fact, this research found that the outcomes associated with young children's nature play (such as connection to nature, stewardship of plants and wildlife, compassionate care for nature, self-confidence, and self-regulation) further the aims of Education for Sustainability (Ernst et al. 2021). (See Box 5.2 for a summary of this research.)

Saving is about the survival of living creatures and other natural elements of Planet Earth. Saving is also about social justice and accepting our grave responsibility to care for our common home. This form of justice – called "ecological justice" (Young 2024) – relates to "right action" as one of the eight laws of Buddhism. "Saving" is thus a spiritual issue grounded in what is morally or ethically right.

Attending to ecological justice indicates that fostering the development of spirituality in the lives of young children means "more than simply being concerned with children feeling happy and good about themselves" (Ellyatt 2024, p. 98). There's a challenging side to eco-spirituality – that is, a calling to act in ways that go beyond our individual self-interests.

Perhaps this calling applies to us as a species as well. Perhaps we need to end the practice of putting human interests before the interests of all other creatures. This practice – referred to as "species-ism" (Bone & Blaise 2015) – reflects hierarchical thinking, where humans are considered to be superior to all other species. This way of thinking – also referred to as "human exceptionalism" – can lead to exploitation of the other-than-human elements of the world.

Post-humanism, or post-humanistic thinking, counteracts the basic premise of species-ism, in that it questions hierarchies and "enables a decentring of the human" (Bone & Blaise 2015, p. 25). "Decentring" opens up "the possibility of being in the world in a different way – "a connected/entangled/knotted way" (Bone & Blaise 2015, p. 18). One application of post-humanism to nature-based early childhood education involves embracing nature as co-teacher, where "the human is de-centered and learning becomes a shared project" (Blenkinsop, Morac & Jickling 2022, p. 40). What we, as humans, can learn from and with nature is far more than what we can ever learn from books. "Like physical affordances, ... the potential for relational lessons from the environment may also be infinite" (Humphreys & Blenkinsop 2018, p. 10).

This shared approach to teaching and learning reflects an "intra-active pedagogy." This pedagogy focuses on "not only taking what is happening between human subjects into consideration, but what is happening between humans and non-humans/objects" (Lindgren 2020, p. 919). An intra-active pedagogy is based on the understanding that agency isn't something limited to humans. It's also based on the understanding that inter-connections occur between different forms of matter making themselves intelligible to each other (Lenz Taguchi 2010). Intra-active pedagogy has relevance for early childhood education for sustainability and is often reflected in efforts to promote both savoring and saving the natural world.

Many early childhood educators would prioritize "savoring" over "saving" in their work with young children but also appreciate the fact that it's not an either/or choice. They're aware that they can focus on both. Additionally, there are ways in which savoring and saving reinforce each other. Savoring the world of nature leads to wanting to protect it. Working to do so often leads to an appreciation of the way nature works *with us* in the conservation and restoration process. Witnessing this form of reciprocity leads us to savoring nature even more. Participation in restoration ("saving") initiatives can also heighten one's spiritual understanding and reverence for nature, as it "encourages feelings of connection to the natural world" (Kellert 2012, p. 106). Through restoration efforts, the human–Earth relationship can be restored as well as the land.

Both savoring and saving the natural world are expressions and promoters of spirituality. They may even be considered forms of praise and gratitude (Armstrong 2023), as both saving and savoring recognize and respect the sacredness of the world in which we live.

I sometimes think of "saving and savoring" the natural world in terms of "a beauty and a burden." Savoring, with a focus on beauty, may have greater appeal than the burden of saving. Yet "burden" isn't just about bearing a heavy load or dealing with a situation that is emotionally difficult. Burden is also defined as a central theme or topic. In a musical context, "burden" refers to a chorus or refrain. In some situations, burden refers to a duty or responsibility. It can also refer to a covenant or solemn agreement.

A covenant can be a beautiful thing, especially if reciprocity is involved. Marriage vows represent a type of covenant, where the spouses make a solemn promise to care for and love each other. The idea of a covenant appears in some religious texts as a promise between God and the human community. "You shall dwell in the land that I gave to your fathers, and you shall be my people, and I will be your God" (English Standard Version Bible 1962, p. 996).

Perhaps we would do well to think of "saving the Earth" as a covenant. We know the Earth takes care of us. Can we commit to caring for the Earth? Can we accept working to "save the Earth" as a responsibility, a central theme, and a refrain appearing in the many facets of our lives?

BOX 5.1 SUGGESTIONS: KNOW YOUR WHY

The roles and responsibilities of professionals working with young children are varied and challenging. To be successful, early childhood educators need to be compassionate, patient, creative, organized, and have strong communication skills. But above all, they need to have a clear understanding of and a strong commitment to the *why* of what they do. Just as organizations and programs need a clear mission to help them accomplish their goals, early childhood professionals need a strong focus on what it is that fuels their work.

Laura Brothwell, the founder and director of Stone Hen Childcare in North Lincolnshire, United Kingdom, when asked about her work, says it's all about the "why." The "why," she said, "is rooted in the spiritual dimensions of connecting children with nature." Laura's goal in establishing Stone Hen was to give young children rich opportunities to experience the magic of nature-based, child-led learning. This meant giving them opportunities to learn, not only in nature, but *with* nature. It meant supporting children's innate curiosity about the natural world, respecting their ability to explore and make meaning of the world around them, giving them opportunities to experience community, and instilling in them a life-long love of learning (Brothwell 2024).

Maintaining a focus on the "why" is probably the most important thing educators can do, to not only deliver excellent programming, but to also experience constant re-fueling of energy and enthusiasm for their work with young children.

Reference

Brothwell, L. (2024). Personal communication, August 19, 2024.

Ecological Perspective Taking

Once given the opportunity to engage deeply with different elements of the natural world, children tend to view nature as kin. This sense of kinship was evident in interviews with a group of five-year-old children after several visits to a forest. The children's responses during the interviews demonstrated empathy (one manifestation of kinship) for plants and animals. They expressed a need to protect the plants and animals of the forest and seemed to enjoy the presence of other living things. Viewing nature as kin was especially evident in one girl's statements about caring for trees: "I care because they have a soul too" (Lithoxoidou et al. 2017, p. 9).

The children's responses after their visits to the forest reflect ecological perspective taking (taking the perspective of other living things) and eco-centric thinking. While young children are sometimes described as being ego-centric (thinking primarily about self), their words and actions demonstrate that they can also be eco-centric (Margoni & Surian 2017). Manifestations of eco-centric dispositions observed in preschool children include interest in the needs of other forms of life, a sense of caring about their welfare, and an appreciation of their intrinsic value (Lithoxoidou et al. 2017). These dispositions reflect spiritual dimensions of connectedness to nature.

A painting by Joseph Wright of Derby provides a dramatic illustration of children's ecological perspective taking. This painting – "An Experiment on a Bird in an Air Pump" – depicts a re-enactment of an experiment to test the existence of oxygen. The experiment is being performed on a small bird, a grey cockatiel. The bird is trapped inside a glass vessel where an air pump is used to extract oxygen. A group of people watch as the bird begins to droop and struggles to breathe as air is pumped out of the vessel. The adults seem interested in the experiment but detached from what the bird is experiencing. They show little sympathy or empathy. The children, however, seem frightened and distressed. One child covers her eyes.

Human curiosity and ingenuity are evident in this painting. Also evident on the part of the adults is an attitude of domination over nature. Such an attitude can easily lead to harmful and unjust exploitation. The experiment depicted in the painting – along with many other scientific experiments conducted with animals – is an example of how an attitude of domination over nature causes harm to other creatures. One such experiment involved removing baby rhesus monkeys from their mothers to study the role of love and affection in the early years (Harlow, Dodsworth, & Harlow 1965).

Whether it's biophilia or some other dimension of connectedness to nature, many young children recognize that being very young warrants special consideration (Bone 2008). The same applies to being very small. One study, based on field observations and staff interviews, indicates that young children are interested in small animals and want to help them (Lerstrup, Chawla, & Heft 2021). Ways in which the children demonstrated care for small animals included gathering grass to make a nest for a small creature and gently helping a dung beetle turn around after he flipped onto its back. Other studies have documented children caring for small plants as well (Argent et al. 2017; Lithoxoidou et al. 2017). One example relates to children singing familiar songs and whispering words of encouragement to "baby trees" (Argent et al. 2017).

Kellert (2012), whose work includes articulating the different dimensions of biophilia, indicates that dominion and exploitation are two of the eight ways in which humans attach meaning to and derive benefits from the natural world. Kellert refers to these eight ways as biophilic values. The other six are attraction, reason, aversion, affection, spirituality, and symbolism. None of these eight biophilic tendencies or values is intrinsically wrong or harmful in itself. How each one is expressed, however, can be destructive.

Dominion, as a biophilic value, reflects the need to control and, at times, master our environment. This need isn't unique to humans. All species seek ways to adapt to their environment. This is required for fitness and survival. Dominion becomes a problem when the inclination to master nature becomes excessive and the needs of the environment are ignored. This, according to Kellert (2012), is what modern society tends to do. We look to nature primarily as a natural resource and undervalue "nature's contribution to our physical, emotional, intellectual, and even spiritual health and well-being" (p. 49).

Robin Wall Kimmerer (2013), in *Braiding Sweetgrass*, proposes a different view. She suggests looking to the natural world as a gift versus a resource. "The currency of a gift economy," she says, "is, at its root, reciprocity" (p. 28). This means that once we receive the gifts of nature, we find a way to "make something beautiful in return" (Kimmerer 2013, p. 152).

Early Childhood Education for Sustainability

Research on early childhood education for sustainability (ECEfS) is gaining momentum (Davis & Elliott 2014; Davis, Elliott & Arlemalm-Hager 2024), as is research on spirituality at the early childhood level (Wills 2025). Reflections on these two areas of interest indicate considerable overlap. Both highlight the importance of kinship, reciprocity, empathy, compassion, mindfulness, and connectedness or relationships. Both also recognize that living well on Planet Earth isn't an individual accomplishment – nor is it just about humans. Living well on the Earth is about interdependence, reciprocity, and respect for the entire ecosystem. Kimmerer (2013) says it more poetically – "Whatever our gift, we are called to give it and to dance for the renewal of the world" (p. 384).

The idea of sustainability at the early childhood level has, at times, been controversial, and one concern focuses on whether or not young children have the capacity to understand the concept. This concern may raise questions about the developmental appropriateness of ECEfS. Another concern relates to how placing the burden of sustainability on the shoulders of young children may be harmful to their mental health. Both of these concerns are based on misunderstandings about ECEfS.

The focus of ECEfS isn't about telling children to "save the earth." In fact, as expressed by international leaders in ECEfS, "education that results in young children becoming 'worriers or warriors' for sustainability is inherently wrong" (Davis & Elliott 2014, p. 2). ECEfS recognizes that children generally have a relational view of the world and thus an intuitive understanding of the principles behind sustainability. These principles are rooted in cognitive, emotional, and spiritual dimensions of nature connectedness (Wills 2025). These principles are also rooted in an understanding of reciprocity.

In a reciprocal relationship, both players exercise agency. They intra-act, often with mutually transformative outcomes. An understanding of intra-action between a child and the rest of the natural world can "liberate ECEfS from its confinement and celebration of the tenet of the agentic child, towards an entangled and relational subject who is constantly co-constituted together with non-human agentic forces" (Weldermariam & Wals 2020, p. 20).

Unfortunately, unsustainability – rather than sustainability – seems to be the default mode of operating in many countries around the world. The other-than-human elements of the natural world tend to be viewed as "goods and services" that exist to meet human "needs and wants" versus humans standing in "right relationship" with them. As Kimmerer (2024) says, "We purchase things we don't really need while destroying things we do need" (p. 72). Obviously, this unsustainable way of living calls for dramatic change. Yet mainstream education – even at the early childhood level – "appears to be eroding basic predispositions for relational caring ways of being in the world" (Wals 2017, p. 158). But it doesn't have to be this way – educational programs can focus on both savoring and saving the natural world.

Empirical research from both ecopsychology and developmental psychology supports the idea of refocusing environmental education in the early years to include education for sustainability (Barrable 2019). The research also suggests that ECEfS should be built around the basic components of (1) sustained contact with nature, (2) engagement with nature's beauty, (3) cultivation of compassion towards all of nature, and (4) mindfulness (Barrable 2019; Barrable et al. 2021). While these components play key roles in ECEfS, they also contribute to young children's spiritual development.

Another aspect of ECEfS that needs to be recognized relates to agency – both the agency of the child and the agency of the other-than-human world. Recognizing the agency of the child addresses concerns relating to the misunderstanding that young children aren't "ready" to be involved in sustainability concerns. Recognizing the agency of the rest of the natural world highlights ways in which other-than-humans are more than "a passive background for humans to act on" (Weldermariam & Wals, p. 13).

BOX 5.2   RESEARCH NOTE: NATURE PLAY AND SUSTAINABILITY

A 2021 research study compared outcomes of young children's nature play with the aims of education for sustainability (EfS) (Ernst et al. 2021). This study included (1) a systematic review of the literature focusing on child development outcomes associated with young children's nature play, and (2) an alignment of the child development outcomes with Education for Sustainability outcomes. The review identified a total of 98 outcomes of nature play, with the most frequently reported outcomes relating to connection to nature, stewardship or care of nature, self-confidence, and self-regulation. The outcomes identified through this literature review were then mapped to early childhood education for sustainability (ECEfS) outcomes, as outlined by the Cloud Institute's Education for a Sustainable Future.

Results of this mapping exercise indicate that nature play supports EfS benchmarks in the areas of applied knowledge, dispositions, skills, and applications. These findings show that "nature play's contribution to sustainability is both extensive and rich" and thus should not be abandoned in the pursuit of sustainability.

Reference

Ernst, J., McAllister, K., Siklander, P. & Storli, R. (2021). Contributions to sustainability through young children's nature play: A systematic review. *Sustainability*, 13, 1–36.

Sustainability and Spirituality

"Saving", in the context of education *for* the environment, is about sustainability. In some people's minds, this could mean saving the Earth so that humans can survive. This focus, however, has been criticized by some scholars for being anthropocentric or human-centered (Wang 2017). Anthropocentric thinking regards humans as the central, or most important, element of existence. This way of thinking reflects a "narrow view of sustainability" and, when applied to education, fails to give learners an authentic understanding of nature (Wang 2017).

A broader view of sustainability education highlights reciprocity and the non-dual relation between the self and the rest of the natural world (Wang 2017). This approach focuses not just on the welfare of humans but on all the elements of the natural world. This non-anthropocentric approach reflects an appreciation of what has been referred to as the "no-self", or the loss of self-preoccupation. "The no-self approximates a spiritual level of selflessness, reminding us that humans should be free of the attitude of egotism. The human 'self' is neither the centre of the universe nor the ruler of its surroundings" (Wang 2017, p. 555).

David Orr, Professor Emeritus of Environmental Studies and Politics at Oberlin College, also links sustainability and spirituality. In writing about the challenges of sustainability, Orr notes how a "higher level of spiritual awareness" may the "most difficult challenge of all" (Orr 2002, p. 1459). This higher level, he says, "honors mystery, science, life, and death" (p. 1459). This higher level also requires a dramatic shift in the way we, as a society, live on Planet Earth. We are currently placing demands on the Earth that are impossible to sustain. We are creating a "spiritually impoverished world" and, in so doing, becoming spiritually impoverished ourselves. "A spiritually impoverished world is not sustainable because meaninglessness, anomie, and despair will corrode our desire to sustain it and the belief that humanity is worth sustaining" (Orr 2002, p. 1457).

Working from a place of "spiritual emptiness" will never take us to a sustainable future. And as Kimmerer (2013) says, "If all the world is a commodity, how poor we grow" (p. 31). It's encouraging to know that some scholars are looking more closely at links between sustainability and spirituality. Their work is built, in part, around the idea that the practice of spirituality is "aligned to social justice, environmental sustainability, as well as economic equity" (Leal Filho et al. 2022, p. 2). Their work is also based on the fact that issues related to spirituality permeate all of the United Nations Sustainable Development Goals (Leal Filho et al. 2022).

A study involving 100 academics working in different disciplines at higher education institutions in 25 countries reported that almost half of the participants (45%) viewed spirituality as a necessary element for sustainability (Leal Filho et al. 2022). Sixty-nine percent agreed that spirituality is instrumental to an understanding of the indivisible connection between the planet and all living organisms, including humans.

Based on the critical need for a sustainable future, Orr calls for dramatic changes in the way we educate our children. "The kind of education needed for the transition to sustainability," he says, "has little to do with improving SAT or GRE scores or advancing skills necessary to an expansionist phase of human culture" (Orr 2002, p. 1459). What's needed, he says, has a lot to do with helping young people develop the understandings, dispositions, and skills needed for living well on the Earth. Promoting this awareness should be one of the primary goals in our work with young children. Dedicated scholars recognize this and have been working for a number of years to raise awareness of the importance of education for sustainability at the early childhood level (Davis & Elliott 2014; Davis, Elliott & Arlemalm-Hager 2024). Scholars have also proposed specific practices that can be used with young children to promote a sustainability mindset (Rodenburg & Dueck 2025). Some such practices focus specifically on babies and toddlers (Kinley & Elliott 2024).

While some people may think that sustainability is not an early childhood issue, there are strong arguments as to why it is. One argument relates to the way in which education for sustainability contributes to the holistic development of young children, including their spiritual development. Unfortunately, the spiritual aspects of sustainability education aren't always recognized. A growing number of scholars are calling attention to this concern (Garrison, Östman & Van Poeck 2024).

Scholars focusing on different aspects of education for sustainability have noted how it overlaps with education for peace (Mische & Harris 2008). Both emphasize respect and care for other living beings. This has been articulated as the colour green being "a 'go' for peace education" (Wilson 2009, p. 40). This argument is based on the understanding that some of the knowledge, skills, and attitudes promoted in peace education are integral to ECEfS. While we usually think of a culture of peace as abiding within a group of people, it can also apply to the relationship between people and the rest of the natural world.

A 2023 document, the UNESCO (United Nations Educational, Scientific and Cultural Organization) *Recommendation on Education for Peace, Human Rights, and Sustainable Development*, provides further insights into the intersection between education for peace and education for sustainability (EfS). The UNESCO document defines peace as more than the absence of violence and conflicts. Peace is described as a process "that nurtures our ability to value human dignity and take care of ourselves, each other, and the planet we share" (UNESCO).

> **BOX 5.3   REFLECTIONS: EDUCATION AS IF PEOPLE AND PLANET MATTERED**
>
> This is what I learned in school: when writing about self, the "I" is always capitalized; but when writing about we, the "w" is never capitalized unless "we" is at the beginning of a sentence. In school, I also learned to analyse and categorize; I learned about synonyms and antonyms – to think in terms of what's the same and what's different. I was tested and graded on knowledge I retained and on skills I could demonstrate. I learned to follow the rules of grammar and to apply the steps of the scientific method. While some of what I learned in school has helped me succeed in life, other lessons have given me a distorted view of the world in which we live.
>
> One of the biggest flaws in my education, as I see it, resides in the use of the capital "I" in reference to self. We use the upper-case form of "I" every time we write about ourselves but use the lower case when writing about a tree or stone or cloud. The capital "I" gets lodged in our psyche as well as in our writings. We become the all-important entity compared with other entities around us. The capital "I" consecrates our individual rights and freedoms, our personal interests and goals, and our subjective views of reality. The capital "I" comes with a big takeover reflected in an "it's-all-about-me" attitude. Once the "I" takes over, there's little room for wholesome growth.
>
> Education as if people and planet matter requires a different attitude, a different view of who we are and how we fit into the larger reality. The "I" needs to step down from centre stage. "We" should be the main attraction, with "we" being all of us – not just humans.
>
> I now realize that some of the most interesting and important aspects of life were never addressed in school.

Categorizing focused my attention on differences and separateness. Textbooks and assignments rarely highlighted sameness and togetherness. I now know that there are amazing similarities between the rings of a tree and the rings of human fingerprints. I've also learned that chimpanzees and humans care for their infants in very similar ways. These and other fascinating realities about the world of nature were rarely discussed in school.

My knowledge base has expanded since I've been out of school and discovering things on my own. Something else has expanded as well – my sense of wonder.

I was asked a lot of "what" questions during my years as a student: What planet is closest to the sun? What do we call trees that shed their leaves once a year? Wonder, however, seemed to have no place in the curriculum. Getting the right answers to the "what" questions did little to enrich my daily life. Wonder, on the other hand, brings more joy to my life than a million facts will ever do.

Wonder takes us outside of ourselves. With wonder, "i" is no longer an upper-case entity. Wonder takes us to a different kind of knowing. School taught me that humans are exceptional beings. Wonder tells me that everything is exceptional. School encouraged me to be the best that I could be. Wonder tells me that we are part of a larger whole and that no one is at their best unless we grow and thrive together.

I was once expected to celebrate *my* accomplishments – the A's on my report card, my graduation from college, my promotion at work, the publication of my first book. The big "I" took pride in what I did. Celebrating such accomplishments is fine – up to a point. There are bigger accomplishments to celebrate: the Earth continues to spin, an acorn becomes a tree, and bees produce honey. There are more meaningful phenomena to consider than whether or not I succeeded in math.

In school, I never learned about kinship with the rest of the natural world. I learned that humans were *Homo sapiens*, a species apart from – and superior to – other primates. What I learned were primarily facts or understandings that could be proven by physical evidence. I respect that kind of knowing but find other ways of knowing equally important to quality of life. Gathering facts about the world is one way to know the world; another way is to develop a relationship with it. "To know" in this sense is "to be aware of" or "to be familiar with." This type of knowing includes the realization that humans and the rest of the natural world co-exist; we live and thrive in relationship with each other. This relationship is built on interdependence. We are eco-sapiens. The "I" may be written as a capital letter, but what it represents is a rather small world. The concept of kinship opens up a much larger world.

For healthy functioning of people and planet, the capital "I" needs to go. We, as humans, can't continue to regard ourselves as superior or exceptional. We, as humans, don't own the planet, we don't govern it, and its purpose isn't to feed our ego or our greed. We are members of the Earth community. This is the message that needs to ring through the halls of learning. We need to view ourselves as ecological beings, not superior beings.

Education as if people and planet matter means replacing the capital "I" with a "We" – at least in our mind. It means eliminating dualistic thinking and minimizing antonyms and categories. It means redefining words in our everyday vocabulary. Words like "progress", "success", "freedom", and "mine" need to take on different meanings. Education as if people and planet matter requires an awareness of a kinship relationship with all the earthly elements.

We might keep the capital "I" in our written language, but we need to expel it from our minds. We need to tear that wall down, as the capital "I" distorts our view of reality. Once we remove this distortion, we'll see that what makes life matter – and what makes it really meaningful – lies beyond the individual self.

> If you've ever released a rehabilitated animal into its natural habitat, you know something about the thrill of stepping outside of yourself. The thrill comes from knowing that the animal you're releasing is getting a second chance at living the life it was meant to live. If we can rehabilitate ourselves, release ourselves from egocentric thinking, we, too, may have a second chance at living the life we are meant to live. Individuals who have taken part in animal rehabilitation programs often describe the moment of release as "exhilarating." Perhaps we, as humans, can experience something similar in releasing ourselves from the confines of the capital "I." Once released, we'll be free to be what we were meant to be. Release from the capital "I" will give both people and planet a chance to thrive.

Conclusion

Education for sustainability (EfS) applies to every level of education, including the early childhood level. The rationale for addressing sustainability when working with young children relates to what is good for children, society, and the Earth. The process includes attention to both savoring and saving the natural world. EfS overlaps with peace education, which promotes harmonious relationships between groups of people and between people with the rest of the natural world. There are reasons to believe that EfS will never achieve its goals without attending to the spiritual dimensions of connectedness to nature.

6
Trail Guide

Maps and Trail Guides

Hikers know the value of maps and trail guides. They look to these resources for information about where they are, where they want to go, and how to get there. A good trail guide includes information about what might be encountered along the way. This chapter is designed to provide a similar service for adults working to promote the spiritual dimensions of young children's connectedness to nature. Portions of this trail are still unexplored, but being aware of facilitators and inhibitors may enhance the journey.

In some instances, a lack of clarity about nature can be an inhibitor to promoting the spiritual components of connectedness to nature (Adams, Bull & Maynes 2016). Limited ideas about how "to be in nature" (Wagenfeld & Marder 2024) and the lack of professional development and pedagogical guidelines for educators are additional inhibitors (Leal Filho et al. 2022). Other inhibitors include entrenched educational practices, consumerism, and human exceptionalism. An awareness of these inhibitors and addressing them in a positive way are important steps in making a program more impactful.

What Is Nature?

Human attitudes and ways of thinking about nature can be either a facilitator or an inhibitor in promoting the spiritual dimensions of young children's connectedness to nature. Appreciating a kinship relationship with nature – as discussed in Chapter 1 – is certainly a facilitator. Misguided ideas about nature – or even the lack of clarity about the meaning of nature – can be an inhibitor. Consider the following: A three-year-old, when asked if she liked nature, responded by saying "I've never been to nature." Her answer reflects the understanding that nature is separate from humans, something to visit or go to. Choices made by adults sometimes suggest a similar belief such as moving out of the city to "get back to nature" or taking a group of children to a city park to "find nature." This doesn't mean that we shouldn't look for more natural places to spend our time. The child's response simply highlights the importance of recognizing that we are part of nature and that the natural world is our natural habitat.

Viewing nature as something "out there" or as "separate from self" serves as a barrier to more spiritual connections with nature. It can also support anthropocentric (human-centred) ways of relating to the natural world, including a great deal of unsustainable behaviours. Anthropocentric ways of relating to nature tend to be more prominent in Western versus Eastern or Indigenous cultures. In very general terms, the Eastern view of nature has traditionally regarded humans and the universe as continually interacting with each other. Indigenous people around the world also tend to view humans and nature as being deeply connected and interdependent (Kimmerer 2024). The Western view tends to consider humans and nature as two separate entities (Acharibasam & McVittie 2023).

A society aligned with the more Western view has been described as a "culture of functioning" (Arvay 2018a). Priorities in such a culture are centred on the economy. The focus is on financial earnings versus spiritual yearnings. Such a culture tends to dismiss the affective and spiritual benefits of nature. This is to our peril, as living detached from nature makes us less

TABLE 6.1 Contrasting Priorities in the Human/Nature Relationship

Culture of functioning	Kinship-based culture
Dominance	Reciprocity
Development	Fulfilment
Using	Co-habiting
Human-centric	Eco-centric
Divisive	United
Individualistic	Collectivist
Gaining	Sharing
Innovation at any cost	Conservation and sustainability

whole, less healthy, and less happy. As outlined in Table 6.1, there are stark differences between the priorities of a culture of functioning and a kinship-based culture. A culture of functioning is more of a "take-what-you-can" culture, whereas a kinship-based culture focuses on co-existence, peace, and reciprocity.

A "culture of functioning" – in addition to being harmful to the environment – can be harmful to the human spirit, in that it works against the spiritual development of individuals and societies. Efforts to promote children's holistic development and to strengthen their spiritual connections with nature can be hindered if the priorities of the community in which they live reflect a culture of functioning. Such a culture builds and rewards performativity-based education systems, which leave little room for aesthetic and spiritual development.

The principles of Forest School differ dramatically from performativity-based education systems. These principles, as outlined in *Forest School and Nature Pedagogy* (Cree & Robb 2021), are based on "harmony with nature" versus "domination of nature." These principles reflect an appreciation of the spiritual values of nature.

The Forest School approach has its roots in the Scandinavian philosophy of Friluftsliv ("free air life"). This lifestyle philosophy includes a deep appreciation of freedom in nature and spiritual connectedness with the land. With the rapid growth of Forest Schools around the world, there are concerns about the institutionalization and commodification of Forest School practices diluting or losing the core components of the Forest

School philosophy (Leather 2018). Even though children in a Forest School program may spend almost the entire school day outdoors, the way they spend their time outdoors may not be consistent with the Forest School philosophy. Additionally, just taking children outdoors doesn't necessarily promote their spiritual connections with nature.

How to Be in Nature

Limited ideas about how "to be in nature" can also be a barrier to deeper connectedness with nature. This concern is addressed by Amy Wagenfeld and Shannon Marder (2024) in their book, *Nature-Based Allied Health Practice*. Related discussion includes a story about Judith Sadora, a licensed marriage and family therapist who established a psychotherapy clinic in Oregon. Judith's work with youth often takes place in nature, which she regards as co-therapist. The nature focus was inspired by her professional background in outdoor behavioural healthcare and her personal experiences in nature.

While Judith's observations of youth and young adults in wilderness therapy programs convinced her of the power of nature to heal and transform lives, she was troubled by the unspoken messages about how to be in nature. Such messages tended to reflect "individualistic and conquering narratives that are easily found in Western Euro-American culture" (Wagenfeld & Marder 2024, p. 45). Her personal experiences as a Nigerian woman, on the other hand, carried a different message. For Judith, "being outside means connection to God, ancestors, and community" (Wagenfeld & Marder 2024, p. 47).

Judith recognized that being outdoors and experiencing the benefits of nature can look different for different people and cultures. She thus chose "culture" as one of the pillars of her work. Her other three pillars are nature, community, and spirituality. Judith recognizes that the first step in helping children, families, and individuals heal their wounds through nature-focused therapy is honouring them and where they are in developing a connectedness with nature. She knows that the way a program works in one community may not be right for another community. The culture and priorities of the community need to be considered. A quote from the poet, Rumi, says it well: "There are a thousand ways to kneel and kiss the ground."

Thus, using a "drag and drop" approach in connecting children with nature through the Forest School model may not work in all communities. The danger in dragging a program from one country or community and dropping it into another country or community comes with the risk of not acknowledging the local place, environment, or culture of that community (Lloyd, Truong & Gray 2018).

The same principle applies to "dragging and dropping" certain strategies in efforts to meet the needs of individual children. What may work for one child may not work for all children in a group. An emergent curriculum, as discussed in Chapter 3, recognizes not only the interests of the group but also the interests, fears, and abilities of each individual child. Some children are afraid of, or uncomfortable around, worms, insects, and bugs. They may not want to get "dirty" or wet. Such fears and concerns should not be dismissed. Understanding fears and concerns may be an important step in helping a child feel comfortable in a natural setting. If overlooked or dismissed, fear and anxiety can become barriers to connectedness to nature and can diminish an individual's chances of having spiritual experiences in nature (Heintzman 2009).

Place-Based Education and Attachment

Place-based education is an alternative to using a "drag and drop" approach (Lloyd, Truong & Gray 2018) and plays a role in promoting the spiritual dimensions of children's connectedness to nature (Boyd 2019; Elliot & Krusekopf 2017, 2018). Place-based education generally includes outdoor learning and becoming familiar with the multiple dimensions of a specific place, including its natural elements, its inhabitants (both human and other-than-human), its history, and stories. The concept of "place," as used in this context, refers to not only a geographic location but also the emotional and cultural attachments to that place.

At times, the "place" in place-based education with young children seems to take on the role of a learning partner as it responds to the children's playful behaviours (Goodenough, Waite & Wright 2020). This form of reciprocity is sometimes referred to as "intra-play." With intra-play, "human and non-human agents participate and mutually define each other" (Armijo-Cabrera 2025, p. 4). This form of interaction reinforces the understanding that "place" in place-based education is more than a stage on which children take on the role of actors.

Researchers, in one study of children playing in a wooded area, paid close attention not only to children's interactions with the natural environment but also to how the place and the natural elements of the place "provoked responses in the young people and responded to children's play" (Goodenough, Waite & Wright 2020, p. 229). The researchers noticed how the way children used the different spaces and related to the different species visibly impacted the trees and terrain. While the children's actions were self-directed, they seemed to be in response to the "plants' invitations." The trees, for example, "appeared to invite young players to climb and enjoy the sensations accompanying being raised up." The intra-play that occurred suggested a partnership between children and the other-than-human environment – a partnership that gave children "valued opportunities to change their emotional mood and [opportunities for the] trees, to grow" (Goodenough, Waite & Wright 2020, p. 228).

Other studies involving several different early childhood programs using a place-based approach found that, in the majority of the settings, children showed a growing awareness, attachment, and love for the place where they lived, played, and learned. In some cases, this awareness and attachment related to both animate and inanimate aspects of the environment. While these attachments included sandstone walls and bees, they also included "a feeling of spiritual connection with the earth itself" (Boyd 2019, p. 990). Most of the case studies used for this research reflect a Forest School philosophy which includes the understanding that children need frequent and consistent experiences with place to develop a positive relationship with the earth (Boyd 2019).

Humans' attachment to the rest of nature is grounded, in part, in our need for nature. We rely on nature for meeting our physical and psychological needs; but as noted by Alexia Barrable (2025), "conceptualising our relationships to nature as one simply predicated on needs …. misses an opportunity to explore our deeper attachment to the natural world" (p. 68). Barrable encourages a re-conceptualization of our relationship to nature based on the infant–parent bond. This re-conceptualization draws attention to the important role "of socialising agents in the building of this attachment and the detrimental effect of disruptions in the human-nature attachment process" (p. 64).

BOX 6.1   REFLECTIONS: ONE WITH NATURE

It's not unusual to find expressions of oneness with the rest of nature in the writings of poets and mystics. It's less common to find such expressions in the academic literature. Yet there are scholars from different disciplines who also recognize this oneness.

Freya Matthews is one example. Matthews, in *The Ecological Self* (1994) (an academic book published 30 years ago), explains how everything in nature is interconnected. The healthy ecological self, she says, identifies self with the universe. Matthews explains how thinking otherwise – that is, to view the universe as fragmented rather than whole – leads to regarding nature as having only instrumental rather than intrinsic value. It also leads humans to act as if they are independent versus interdependent beings.

The work of a growing number of scholars today reinforces the idea of interdependence and oneness. This work highlights the need for a "de-centering of self" as a way to enhance our understanding of the world and to promote compassion for others (both human and the other-than-human). Some of this work is referred to as post-humanism, which involves a de-centering of the human in the human/nature relationship. Post-humanism rejects the idea that humans are separate from or superior to the rest of the natural world. If focuses, instead, on interdependence or oneness. Post-humanism is also embedded in "common worlds" thinking, which recognizes that humans, materials, places, and non-human species share indivisible worlds (Nxumalo & Pacini-Ketchabaw 2017).

An understanding of interdependence and a de-centering of the self may be necessary for the realization of a sustainable future. This understanding makes awe-inspiring experiences in nature especially important, as such experiences can help us de-centre the self and deepen feelings of oneness and connectedness with the world of nature.

Place-Based Education and Agency

Place-based education often includes opportunities for children to play a meaningful role in promoting ecologically sustainable practices in their community. One example from Australia (Konerman et al. 2021) involved a group of preschoolers noticing differences in the health of two connecting ponds – one pond had clear water with native tadpoles thriving; the other was full of algae and home to a non-native fish species. This fish (the Gambusia fish) had been introduced in New South Wales over a century ago in an attempt to control the mosquito population. Through microscopic inspection and pondside observations, the children learned to differentiate between the different species of fish. They also noticed how the Gambusia fish were preying upon native frog tadpoles. The children brainstormed ideas about what they could do to help the native frogs One idea was to build a wall between the ponds.

In addition to addressing the Gambusia fish dilemma, the children decided to do something about the litter they discovered around the ponds. They knew that litter – like non-native fish – can disrupt the ecological balance. The teacher listened to the children's concerns and supported them in developing a plan and a course of action. They picked up litter, designed trash containers that could protect birds from the garbage inside, and wrote and illustrated messages urging the community to be more involved in caring for the ecosystems in their community (Konerman et al. 2021).

The children's active engagement throughout this place-based project promoted several critical process skills, including observation, negotiation, and problem-solving. The children's active engagement also promoted key ecological concepts fundamental to sustainability. As researchers involved with this project explained, "It's all about balancing and belonging" (Elliott & Pugh 2020, p. 205).

This is just one example of young children acting as agents of change in their community. Examples from other communities tell similar stories. These stories and related research show that young children can construct their own knowledge and be active participants in the communities in which they live and learn (Cerino 2021; Chawla 2009).

A review of the literature found that promoting agency in young children is of major importance for education for sustainable development (Bascope, Perasso & Reiss 2019). It's also of major importance in promoting a child's ecological identity and sense of efficacy (Ernst et al. 2021). Finally, providing young children opportunities to act as agents of change recognizes and respects their basic right to do so. This right is articulated in the United Nations Convention on the Rights of the Child, which refers to children as citizens who possess the right of participation. As stated in Article 12 of the Convention, "children have the right to express their ideas and to be heard in matters affecting them" (United Nations 1989).

BOX 6.2   SUGGESTIONS: PROMOTING CHILDREN'S AGENCY

A preschool in Greece involved a group of four-year-old children in planning and creating a more natural playspace on their schoolgrounds. The goal was not only to connect children to nature but to explore the potential of young children being active participants in improving their immediate environment. The organizers of the project found ways to have the children meaningfully involved throughout the entire planning and implementation process.

During the planning phase, the children shared their ideas about what they wanted in the playspace through photos, drawings, conversations during walks around the schoolground, and during group discussions. Adults then worked with the children in developing a scale model of the playspace and presenting this to the school community. Children's ideas for improving the schoolgrounds included adding natural elements (water, soil) and other living beings (trees, flowers, dogs, birds, snails, fish, ants). During the implementation phase, the children were involved in planting flowers, constructing bird feeders, and providing food and water for animals.

Throughout the project, children showed an instinctive interest in and strong feelings for plants, animals, and natural elements. A research component of the project showed that children's involvement promoted greater environmental awareness and reinforced the idea that young children can be empowered to plan and implement meaningful changes to their environment (Tsevreni & Tigka 2018).

Insights gained from this project led to the development of recommendations for a place-based approach to environmental education with young children. As applied to the naturalization of an everyday playspace, these recommendations include the following:

1. Provide child-friendly opportunities for children to share their ideas about what they want in the playspace versus working from fixed, pre-existing plans.
2. Give children both the opportunity and responsibility to create circumstances for connecting with other-than-human nature. Examples include involving children in the care of plants and animals and giving them opportunities to play with such natural elements as soil and water in environmentally responsible ways.

3. Work from a child-focused approach with interested adults (teachers, school staff, administrators, and parents) serving as mentors and guides.

Reference

Tsevreni, I. & Tigka, A. (2018). Young children claiming their connection with nonhuman nature in their schoolground. *Children, Youth & Environments 28*(1), 119–127.

The Spiritual Component

A clear and shared vision of what a program or organization wants to accomplish is an important contributor, or facilitator, to the success of the program or organization. The vision sets the trajectory for what a program or organization becomes. While clarity of vision is an important factor, so is commitment to the vision. This commitment needs to be shared by all members of the team and be evident in the culture of the institution. Explicitly acknowledging the spiritual aspects of nature connectedness in the vision and culture of an organization can contribute greatly to the accomplishment of related goals.

Excerpts from a description of the SOL [Soulful Outdoor Learning] Forest School in New Mexico provide examples of how to make the spiritual dimensions of the program more evident. SOL's stated vision is to connect young children "to the awe & wonder of the natural world"; its mission, "to grow caring, resilient, soulful young humans and future stewards of the Earth." SOL also recognizes children's basic rights – "the right to the solace, serenity, silence, and solitude that is offered in nature" (https://www.solforestschool.com/).

Defining the spiritual dimension of nature-based programming for young children is far from easy, yet not doing so can lead to an over-emphasis on procedures – on the "what" we do versus the "why." Nature-based programs with a spiritual emphasis are guided more by understandings than by directives, more by principles and philosophy than program requirements. This means that they are guided by the "why" of what they do. This "why" should be evident in the pedagogy (the approach to teaching) as well as the physical environment.

The pedagogy of most nature-based programs for young children supports child-initiated learning through practices that prioritize creativity, philosophical thinking, ecological perspective taking, and mindfulness. These practices all have a spiritual component.

A program's philosophy should be evident in the physical environment as well as in the teaching practices. The features of the physical environment make a difference in what the children experience. The experience of learning in a natural environment differs from what is experienced in a human-built environment. This difference may be attributed to biophilia. Children – like the rest of us – are drawn to nature-rich environments. Such environments invite curiosity and wonder – ideal dispositions for learning and for promoting a child's spiritual development.

Children don't develop a view of nature or a relationship with nature in isolation. Their connectedness to nature is, in fact, "a function of a tangle of factors" (Beery, Chawla & Levin 2020, p. 13). The primary factors consist of sociocultural influences, positive time in nature, and interaction with animals. The sociocultural influences include the messages that children receive about nature from parents and other adults and even the way that the physical environment and the rest of society are structured. Such messages can "either encourage children to value nature as part of their emerging identity, or identify themselves as separate from nature" (Beery Chawla & Levin 2020, p. 12).

Messages from the society in which they live can also orient children to thinking about the natural world as something to exploit. Thus, the words that we use in talking about nature play a role in shaping children's understanding about nature. "As long as we frame a worldview with language that refers to the wild as a commodity, it will be treated as one" (Haupt 2021, p. 154). Using technology-based metaphors to explain nature can also be damaging. For example, referring to the Earth as a spaceship or the fungi in soil as a type of internet, "unwittingly invites us to see the natural world as other-than-alive" (Haupt 2021, p. 154). These images of the natural world can erode or diminish children's emotional attachment to nature.

Initiatives to connect (or re-connect) children with nature can be found in many areas of society, including education and other cultural institutions, physical and mental health programs, landscape design projects, and recreation and leisure programs. The focus and components of these programs differ widely. Some emphasize sustainability; others focus more on outcomes related to personal well-being. A number of these programs also have a spiritual component, whether explicitly stated or not.

In some cases, the spiritual component will focus on justice with efforts to make the benefits of nature accessible to everyone. A justice focus may also take the form of animal rights' initiatives and respect for the interdependent web of all existence. The spiritual component may show up in the way certain dispositions (e.g., sensitivity to others) and actions (e.g., acts of kindness) are promoted and the type of opportunities provided (e.g., creative expression). Manifestations of spirituality in a program may include an atmosphere of peace and calm, beauty in the environment, empathy towards other-than-human beings, celebrations of nature's wonders, and expressions of joy.

Conclusion

Messages received from the culture in which we live play a key role in shaping our understandings about nature and how we, as humans, relate to nature. These messages can facilitate or hinder efforts to promote the spiritual dimensions of young children's connectedness to nature. Human-centred messages tend to inhibit these efforts; kinship-centred messages facilitate the efforts. Other inhibitors to the process include limited opportunities for professional development and the lack of pedagogical guidelines. Facilitators include a clear and shared vision about desired outcomes, recognizing children as agents of change, and interactions with animals. Elements of place-based education can also serve as facilitators. Reflections of a spiritual orientation in efforts to deepen young children's connectedness to nature include a focus on interdependence or oneness versus separateness. All adults working with young children would do well to understand the complex factors that play a role in shaping children's attitudes and behaviours in relation to the rest of the natural world.

7

A Proposed Framework

Connectedness to Nature

The past decade has seen tremendous growth in research on children's connectedness to nature. Summaries of many of the related studies can be accessed through the Children & Nature Network Research Library (https://research.childrenandnature.org/). These studies show that increased access to nature can support children in becoming healthier, happier, smarter, and better stewards of the environment.

The importance of engagement with and connectedness to nature applies to people of all ages. Some research, however, suggests that children's connectedness to nature and the role it plays in their holistic development differ in some ways from those of adults. This may be especially true for preschool-age children. Researchers focusing on the uniqueness of young children's connectedness to nature note that "early childhood from two to five years deserves a distinct place in the literature" (Beery, Chawla, & Levin 2020, p. 16). This isn't especially surprising in that the broader literature on human development recognizes the uniqueness of the early years in relation to how children learn and develop.

This uniqueness is typically reflected in the way early childhood education programs focus on the development of the whole child versus academic learning. A whole-child focus usually includes attention to the major domains of child development: physical, cognitive, social, emotional, and linguistic development. One area that has not received as much attention is the development of the ecological self, which basically means an individual's connections with and attitudes towards the natural environment. This aspect of development – like other aspects of child development – can expand over time. More attention to this area of development has much to offer both the child and the rest of the natural world (Humphreys & Blenkinsop 2018).

As discussed in Chapter 2, another area of child development not always addressed in the academic literature is spiritual development. This area, too, can develop over time. Spiritual development and the development of the ecological self often overlap and may reinforce each other.

Ecological Identity and Spiritual Development

The development of a child's ecological identity is influenced by a number of factors, including where the child lives and plays, cultural activities and values, and educational experiences. The development of a child's ecological identity can include growth in spirituality. One of the most important factors in developing a healthy ecological identity is sustained contact with nature. This can lead to a sense of oneness with the rest of the natural world and thus contribute to the child's spiritual development.

Being immersed in nature is more than a pleasant way to spend one's time. A number of individuals who have written their ecological autobiography share stories about how time in nature helped shape their understanding about self and the world around them. Susan is one such individual.

Susan was a student in one of my university-level environmental education courses. Course content included concepts related to ecological identity and how a sense of who we are in relation to the rest of the natural world is developed over time. I introduced the idea of writing an ecological autobiography as a way to explore one's own ecological identity. I defined an ecological autobiography as a narrative or story about one's own experiences and relationship with the rest of the natural world. As a related assignment, I asked the students to write an ecological autobiographical essay describing one of their nature-related experiences and what this experience meant to them. After completing this assignment, many of the students willingly shared their experiences with the rest of the class. They seemed to find meaning in the telling of their stories and hearing about the experiences of the other students.

Susan approached me after class one day and asked if she could do an independent study which would include writing her own ecological autobiography. I agreed to work with her and gave her the additional assignment of keeping a journal throughout the process to record her reflections along the way. Her final report started with the statement, "It was good for my soul."

In writing her ecological autobiography, Susan identified four stages in the development of her ecological identity from early childhood through young adulthood: Nature my playground, Nature my classroom, Nature my responsibility, and Nature my friend. Nature, to Susan during her early years, was a place to play. She and her friends spent hours "playing in the woods, hunting critters, and getting dirty." As she got a little older – during her elementary years – Susan discovered that nature was a place to learn. One of the things she discovered was that, to be a successful hunter of salamanders, you had to know which rocks and logs had "salamander potential." As she described the lessons she learned, Susan noted how "there were many teachers along the way, few of them human and some of them not living at all." She was, of course, referring to the other-than-human elements of the natural world.

In describing the next stage of her relationship with nature, Susan explained how her feelings for nature moved beyond simple enjoyment and fascination to a sense of responsibility. This stage started sometime after adopting Penny, a snapping turtle, from its natural habitat. Susan kept Penny in various fish bowls and aquariums over a period of ten years. "Caring for Penny", she said, "taught me the importance of taking responsibility for the ways in which we disrupt the natural world.... I had altered her natural life and was therefore responsible for making the most of it." When Susan left for college, she asked her mother to take care of Penny. Her mother, a special education teacher, brought Penny to school where she received plenty of attention and continued to serve as a teacher. The following summer, however, when there were no school children around, Susan's brother released Penny back into the wild. Susan was concerned that Penny might not make it through the winter. In her ecological autobiography, Susan wrote, "Though Penny served as a valuable lesson in responsibility, I still think of her and regret having tampered with her wildness at all."

In the fourth stage of her ecological identity development, Susan refers to nature as her friend. She says, "I have reached a point where I can honestly say that I see Nature as a close friend." Susan's relationship to nature as a close friend is consistent with the idea of a kinship relationship, as discussed earlier.

Kinship with nature, as described in the academic literature, is linked to a sense of oneness rather than a distinction between nature and humans (Arola et al. 2023). Comments from a primary-age child indicate that even young children can experience this sense of oneness – "It was like I was not a person, it was like I was the nature." This child had been participating in an "Arts-in-Nature" project focusing on environmental awareness, sustainable behaviours, and child well-being. All of the participating children lived in areas of high deprivation, placing them at risk for optimal child development. Evaluations conducted after the program showed greater connectedness with nature and an enhanced sense of well-being (Moula, Walshe & Lee 2023).

> **BOX 7.1 REFLECTIONS: ECOLOGICAL SELF/SPIRITUAL SELF**
>
> I've been a journal writer for many years. I usually start my day by reflecting on where I am in life, what's going on in the world around me, and on ideas or issues that seem important at the moment. I then record some of my thoughts in what I refer to as a "spiritual journal."
>
> For many years, I've also been interested in the human/nature connection, especially in my own sense of

connectedness with nature. To explore the deeper dimensions of what nature means to me, I decided to write my ecological autobiography. I didn't get far into the writing process when I discovered a great deal of overlap between what I was writing in my spiritual journal and how I was describing my relationship with nature. Both included descriptions of how I experienced awe in nature, how I looked to nature as a source of wonder and inspiration, and how I yearned for a greater awareness of oneness with nature.

I realized, as I wrote my ecological autobiography, how much nature has meant to me over the many years of my life and how my connectedness to nature was an integral part of my spirituality. I also discovered that my connectedness to nature is a dependable strength that I can turn to in times of stress. Perhaps the most important insight I gained from reviewing my journal entries over the years is that my spiritual self and my ecological self aren't two separate dimensions of who I am.

A journal entry from 1974 focuses on how nature, for me, was far more than a resource to sustain my physical life. In that entry, I express a yearning for living in closer communion with nature. I knew it was there for me, and I wanted to respond to its call. Twenty years later, a journal entry dated October 12, 1994, reminds me of how I could always count on nature to be there for me. I wrote, "Nature to me is a companion, very present, close, and influential. Nature guides and graces my way through life…. Nature has been there for me during the major decision-making moments of my life. Nature nurtures me, heals me, thrills me."

Twenty years after that, I was still looking to nature as a dependable strength. In a journal entry dated August 13, 2014, I wrote "Beauty feeds my soul – especially beauty in nature…. One thing that remains constant is my love for nature. I'm fascinated by nature, nurtured by nature, and always drawn to nature."

I was 31 years old when I made the 1974 journal entry. I'm now 82. A few months ago (August 5, 2024), my journal

> entry started with a question: What do I do when I get up in the morning? Here's how I answered that question –
>
> *I marvel at the newness of the day and the possibilities and wonders I may encounter. I offer praise and thanksgiving for the gifts each day brings. I know the world is more than just a thrill or a resource. I know the world is more than a problem to be solved. I know it is filled with mystery and generosity. I know it is a "divine milieu." I am in awe, and I am at peace.*

Charting the Path

Supporting children in developing a sense of kinship with nature requires more than teaching them about nature or just telling them to "go play outdoors." It requires intentionality. Some scholars note how promoting kinship requires a shift from a focus on environmental education to education for sustainability (Barrable 2019). Such a shift retains what is typically included in environmental education (i.e., education *in and about the environment*) but adds a strong focus on sustainability (i.e., education *for the environment*).

Alexia Barrable, a researcher from Scotland, developed a model for early childhood education for sustainability which includes the idea of kinship. This model – which Barrable refers to as a "pedagogy of connection" – includes four key components: sustained contact with nature, engagement with nature's beauty, cultivation of compassion towards non-human nature, and mindfulness (Barrable 2019). Barrable's model is consistent with the framework offered in this book as a guide for fostering the spiritual dimensions of nature connectedness. However, a fifth key component – active engagement – is added to Barrable's model. The following discussion addresses each of these five key components.

Sustained Contact with Nature

Both research and theory support the idea that, for most people, sustained contact with nature tends to enhance their sense of connectedness with nature. Findings from the related research indicate that adults with higher nature connectedness spent more time in natural areas during their childhood than those with lower levels of nature connectedness (Broom 2017; Ward Thompson, Aspinall & Montarzino 2008). Understandings based on theory – especially attachment theory – are consistent with these research findings.

While the well-documented concept of attachment theory is usually discussed in relation to infants becoming emotionally attached to the significant people in their lives, it has also been applied to ways in which young children's attachments expand beyond humans to include animals, places, and nature (Barrable 2025). Whether the attachment is with humans or with other elements of nature, sustained contact plays an important role in the attachment process (Christian 2020).

Attachment to place (topophilia) can also impact children's connectedness to nature, their overall well-being, and their sense of identity (Jack 2010). In this context, it's important to note that "place" and "space" are not the same. The difference can be explained in relation to the extent to which humans have given meaning to a specific area. "Space" is more abstract than "place." "Space" lacks substantial meaning. "Place", on the other hand, is filled with meaning. "Place comes into existence when people give meaning to a part of the larger, undifferentiated space in which they live" (Jack 2010, p. 757).

While we can gain abstract knowledge about a place in a short amount of time, coming to know a place requires spending time in and with that place. Establishing a relationship with a place usually occurs only after we get a "feel" for it and spending some time interacting with it. Jon Cree and Marina Robb (2021) note in *The Essential Guide to Forest School and Nature Pedagogy* how "place attachment or knowing a place is often underestimated" (p. 54). They refer to place attachment as one of the key elements of Forest School.

Sustained contact with a place helps us appreciate the physical and spiritual dimensions of that place, leading to a sense of intimacy – or "kithship" – with that place. "Kithship" is described as "intimacy with the landscape in which one dwells and is entangled" (Haupt 2021, p. 26). While the concepts of kinship and kithship are closely related and interact with each other, there are differences between the two. "Where kin are relations of *kind*; kith is relationship based on *knowledge* of place …. its landmarks, its fragrance, the habits of its wildlings" (Haupt 2021, p. 26).

Active Engagement with Nature

The connectedness to nature research indicates that, while sustained contact plays an important role in establishing a strong bond with nature, it may not be sufficient. One study (Broom 2017) supporting this idea explored associations between young adults' views of and actions towards the environment with their early childhood experiences in nature. Survey responses from 50 study participants showed that participants who played in nature identified themselves as lovers of nature, while those who did not play in nature did not identify themselves as such. Those who loved nature also stated that they wanted to take care of it.

These findings suggest that early and playful childhood experiences in nature may provide formative opportunities for individuals to develop a strong attachment to nature. The findings of this research study also suggest that growing up surrounded by nature (as in rural areas) may not be sufficient to foster deep connections with nature. Contact with nature may need to be paired with reflection, active engagement, and empowerment.

This research and other studies indicate that it's not just being in nature that counts. It's being actively involved with nature. For young children, this usually takes the form of play. (See Chapter 8 for more information about nature play and how it can enhance a child's connectedness to nature.)

Engaging with Nature's Beauty

Beauty is sometimes described as a pathway to nature (Cree & Robb 2021; Lumber, Richardson & Sheffield 2017). Beauty can also be a pathway to spirituality, in that it awakens our sense of wonder and allows us to experience self-forgetting moments of joy and ecstasy (Johnson 2002). And as Barrable (2019) notes, "The aesthetic appeal of nature plays an important role in promoting a connection with the natural world" and "should, therefore, be a focus of a pedagogy for connection" (p. 4). (See Chapter 11 for a further discussion about the importance of engaging with nature's beauty and ideas on how to do this through the creative arts.)

Cultivation of Compassion towards Non-Human Nature

One of the manifestations of children's spirituality is referred to by Tobin Hart (2006) as "relational spirituality." As noted in Chapter 3, manifestations of relational spirituality in children include a sense of caring and compassion. Chapter 5 includes reference to compassion as an essential part of early childhood education for sustainability. While caring for the other-than-human aspects of nature seems to come naturally to young children, competing forces can diminish this tendency. Early childhood is recognized as a key time to nurture this aspect of human development so that it can be strengthened and maintained throughout one's life (Barrable 2019).

Mindfulness

Mindfully engaging with nature tends to promote compassion for other-than-human aspects of nature (Barrable 2019). This, in turn, strengthens nature connectedness and encourages pro-environmental behaviours. Research suggests that mindfulness in nature can also foster pro-social behaviours and emotional regulation (Howell et al. 2011). "Finally, engaging with nature mindfully could have the desired effect in providing the skills to appreciate nature's beauty more deeply" (Barrable 2019, p. 5). (See Chapter 9 for a further discussion about how nature-based mindfulness practices can support the spiritual development of young children.)

BOX 7.2   RESEARCH NOTE: HIGH-IMPACT EXPERIENCES

Not all experiences in nature have the same impact on children's nature connectedness and spirituality. The term "significant nature situations" is sometimes used in reference to experiences with high impact. The question of what makes a nature-related experience "significant" – or what constitutes a "connecting" nature experience for children – was addressed in a study by Matteo Giusti et al. (2018).

Giusti and colleagues interviewed 26 practitioners in the field of connecting children to nature. They asked the practitioners to identify qualities that make a nature situation significant for fostering children's nature connectedness. Qualities identified by the practitioners included "engagement of senses", "mindfulness", "awe", "restorative", "thought-provoking", and "animal engaging."

The practitioners were also asked to share ideas about how to enhance children's connectedness to nature. Their responses highlighted the importance of relating to nature not as an abstract concept but as a natural physical space. They also suggested that a model for promoting children's nature connectedness should include three consecutive phases: being in nature, being with nature, and being for nature. They noted how children need to feel at ease and comfortable in the natural elements of the outdoors before developing concern for the environment and feeling responsible and motivated to act for it. The practitioners also indicated that a sense of connectedness with nature includes seeing oneself as being one with nature. This, they said, involves "a sense of profound personal attachment to nature that can be described as spiritual" (Giusti et al. 2018, p. 9).

Reference

Giusti, M., Svane, U., Raymond, C.M. & Beery, T.H. (2018). A framework to assess where and how children connect to nature. *Frontiers in Psychology, 8*, 2283.

Following the Path

The framework for promoting nature connectedness and spirituality in young children, as presented in this book, emphasizes the importance of learning in nature, about nature, and for nature. It also emphasizes the importance of *being with* nature, promoting an eco-spiritual consciousness, and attending to different pathways.

Being with Nature

"Being with" requires more than being physically present. "Being with" involves "being fully present", where body, mind, and spirit are all engaged. "Being with" also involves kinship, connectedness, and an "I-Thou" relationship – all core components of a framework for promoting the spiritual dimensions of young children's connectedness to nature.

"Being with" nature is also an essential part of the Forest School philosophy. This idea is highlighted by Cree and Robb (2021) in *The Essential Guide to Forest School and Nature Pedagogy*. They note how nature pedagogy means "more than embracing the natural world as a living classroom" (p. 86). It means being with nature in a harmonious way. This involves gratitude, reflection, and compassion.

Promoting an Eco-Spiritual Consciousness

One of the goals of nature pedagogy is the development of an "eco-spiritual consciousness" – that is, "a manifestation of the spiritual connection between human beings and the environment" (Lincoln 2000, p. 227). Research suggests that this spiritual connection is manifested in five essential ways: tending (caring), dwelling (based on meaning and purpose), reverence (based on a sense of the sacred), connectedness (kinship), and sentinence (finding beauty and enchantment) (Lincoln 2000).

Pathways to Nature Connectedness

Richardson et al. (2020) propose a five-pathway model for promoting nature connectedness. This model involves the senses, emotion, beauty, meaning, and compassion. This model is consistent with the framework presented in this book for promoting the spiritual dimensions of young children's connectedness to nature (see Table 7.1).

TABLE 7.1 Framework for Promoting the Spiritual Dimensions of Young Children's Connectedness to Nature*

Key components	Pathways	Activities & experiences	Child outcomes	Nature's contributions
Sustained contact with nature	Being *in* nature	Sensory engagement Embodied experiences	Familiarity with nature Comfort in nature Haptic rapport Place attachment	Repeated refrains Diversity Comfort/healing Generosity
Active engagement with nature	Immersion Sensory experiences Physical interactions Emotional engagement Cognitive engagement Reciprocity	Nature play Close observation Manipulation	Sentience Curiosity Imagination Agency	Affordances Reciprocity
Engagement with nature's beauty	Emotion Noticing nature's beauty Heightened awareness	Art Music Drama Poetry Stories/myths	Awe Joy Happiness Wonder Transcendence	Vastness Inspiration Beauty
Compassion	Relational spirituality	Tending (*being for* nature) Conservation Interacting with plants & animals	Empathy Perspective taking Kinship	Reciprocity
Mindfulness	Dwelling (*being with* nature) Relational spirituality Reverence/sacredness Connectedness Interdependence Oneness Meaning Mystery	Being present Philosophical thinking Wondering	Gratitude Wonder Inner peace Sense of belonging Sense of calm Kinship Positive ecological identity Meaning Wisdom	Generosity Connectedness Guidance Resilience

* Adapted from Barrable's pedagogy of connection (2019).

Conclusion

Connectedness to nature and spirituality share certain characteristics and influence the development of each other. Goals in the development of each include compassion, wonder, a sense of oneness, and an appreciation of interdependence. Pathways to achieving these goals include deep engagement with nature, mindfulness, and meaningful opportunities to actively care for the environment. "Being with" nature plays an important role in the process. A focus on "being with" nature, then, should be considered an essential part of efforts to foster the spiritual dimensions of young children's connectedness to nature.

8

Nature Play

Lost Opportunity

It's with a bit of sadness and regret that I recall an evening walk with my two preschool daughters many years ago. We were near a pond near our home when my five-year-old daughter asked if we could take our shoes off and put our feet in the water. I responded by saying, "Not now. Let's just keep walking." After we got home and the girls were in bed, I thought about my response. If I had been a child, putting my feet in the water would be a lot more fun than "just keep walking."

I remember a time from my own childhood when running barefoot through puddles in our yard was such a joyful experience. Why did I tell my daughter "no"? Perhaps it was because I had an agenda in my head. We left the house to go for a walk. My daughter had no such agenda. She was listening to an invitation from the pond. There was something about the water that seemed to be calling to her.

In academic language, we might call the water an "affordance," something in the environment that seems to invite interaction. That's what my daughter wanted to do. She was far more tuned in to the possibilities of interacting with nature than I was. My agenda focused on walking *through* nature. She wanted to be *with* nature. Her connectedness to nature was something she felt; it was something I was thinking about.

Adults and young children often differ in the way they relate to nature. Young children are in their bodies; adults tend to be in their heads. Young children being "in their bodies," however, involves more than a physical engagement with the material world. Children are naturally curious. Their minds are eager to be engaged, as well. So, too, their spirits, which are fuelled by wonder and imagination. Children not only observe and touch; they also experiment and ponder. Children's way of being in and interacting with the world is especially evident when they're engaged in play, particularly in nature play. It's a mistake to deny children the opportunity to interact deeply and often with the world of nature.

Nature Play

Play isn't a frill for children; it's a necessity for healthy child development. Play, as described by the American Occupational Therapy Association, is the primary occupation of childhood. It's "an inherent process that helps children feel competent and confident" (Wagenfeld & Kennedy 2024, p. 39). Children need play to reach their potential in all areas of development: social, emotional, cognitive, and physical. Play also supports the spiritual development of young children, in that it provides "opportunities to experience spiritual moments, defined as feeling wonder, awe, joy, and inner-peace" (Mata-McMahon 2019, p. 44).

If given the freedom to play, young children usually find ways to play in almost any environment. Certain environments, however, are more conducive to play than others, with natural environments being at the top of the list for creative play. "Almost without fail, natural and unplanned environments have proven to be the richest and most satisfying ways to accomplish play" (Wagenfeld & Kennedy 2024, p. 40). One reason for this relates to the affordances available in natural environments.

As noted earlier, affordances are elements or characteristics of the environment that invite – or "afford" – interaction. Affordances offer meaningful action possibilities. While such possibilities are often viewed in relation to inanimate entities (sticks, hills, water, etc.) and the opportunities such entities provide for physical activities (digging, climbing, splashing, etc.), affordances can also be animate entities, such as small animals (chickens, worms, etc.). Young children are usually fascinated by small animals and willingly become engaged in first-hand activities with them. These activities can take the form of searching for and finding wild creatures, catching and releasing them, and acting out such animal roles as building nests and climbing trees (Lerstrup, Chawla & Heft 2021). As mentioned in Chapter 3, affordances can be people, too.

Nature play – that is, play in natural environments and with natural materials – can take many different forms, but at its core is an interaction between the child and nature. The interaction may range from close observation to such risk-taking activities as climbing high, walking down a steep incline, or holding a wriggly worm. Nature play involves playing *with nature*, not just in nature.

One form of nature play is referred to as "bio play" which consists of exploratory-active play involving plants, wildlife, and care. Bio play is one of nine primary play types included on the *Tool for Observing Play Outdoors* (TOPO). This tool provides an observational framework that can be used for studying child-initiated outdoor play and for evaluating the play environment itself (Loebeck & Cox 2020). A study using TOPO to assess young children's outdoor play behaviours in naturalized play environments found that gardening areas with a variety of loose parts offered significant opportunities to participate in both exploratory and bio play (Ramsden et al. 2025).

Nature play is not just any type of play in an outdoor environment. Playing soccer according to the "rules of soccer," for example, is not nature play. Rolling a soccer ball down a hill or trying to sink a soccer ball in a tub of water can be considered forms of nature play, in that the processes involved allow children to be active participants in the way nature works. Gravity pulls the soccer ball down the hill. Density keeps the ball from staying under water. Children experimenting with these forces of nature can make exciting discoveries.

While nature play can lead to scientific discoveries about the way nature works, other outcomes are equally important. Such outcomes include the joy of rich sensory experiences and the wonder often associated with such experiences. Nature play offers the potential for whole-body engagement, the challenge of taking risks, and the opportunity for self-directed inquiry. These characteristics make nature play especially attractive to a curious, creative, and risk-taking child. The open-endedness of the affordances in natural environments provides a "goodness of fit" for young children at play, including children with differing abilities.

Natural environments and natural materials come richly endowed with play potential. They invite "authentic play", which is the best kind of play for young children. Authentic play is open-ended and freely chosen. The rewards of nature play are intrinsic rewards – no trophies, no winners and losers, no conforming to human-made rules – just joy, personal satisfaction, discovery, excitement, and a sense of efficacy. Additional benefits of nature play identified through research include enhanced connectedness to nature, boosts in brain development, stronger social bonds, and reduced stress (Johnstone et al. 2022; Kiewra & Veselack, 2016). Nature play also promotes the spiritual development of young children, as evidenced by joy, wonder, creativity, and deeper connections with nature.

BOX 8.1 RESEARCH NOTE: NATURE PLAY REMEMBERED

Scandinavian countries have a tradition of being outdoors for play, learning, and relaxation. This tradition is often referred to as "friluftsliv", which combines the Norwegian words for free, air, and life. The friluftsliv tradition emphasizes the simplicity and richness of outdoor living as a pathway to well-being.

A related research study (Fasting & Høyem 2024) investigated ways in which eight young Norwegian adults (age 24) remembered their friluftsliv experiences from childhood. Individual walking interviews were used to collect information for this study. The interviews were conducted in natural settings where the interviewees played as children. As they walked, the young adults were asked to reflect upon their friluftsliv-related childhood experiences and memories.

All eight interviewees highlighted "wonder, creativity and curiosity as important parts of their childhood experiences outdoors" (p. 152). They described how these feelings or characteristics "blossomed while playing in natural surroundings" (p. 152). The interviewees related their feelings of joy and wonder to the sense of freedom they experienced in the outdoor environment and described how movements and feelings were related. They described how positive feelings were activated when given the freedom to do what they chose to do during outdoor play. For them, the joy of movement was experienced as something physical, emotional, and social and in relation to the surroundings. The young adults also indicated that their childhood experiences in nature "have become important parts of who they are today" (p. 145).

Reference

Fasting, M. L. & Høyem, J. (2024). Freedom, joy and wonder as existential categories of childhood – reflections on experiences and memories of outdoor play. *Journal of Adventure Education and Outdoor Learning, 24*(2), 145–158.

Being and Becoming

Nature play for the young child can be discussed in relation to "being" and "becoming" (Beery, Chawla & Levin 2020), both of which play a role in the spiritual development of the child. "Being", in this context, generally refers to the young child's experience of both "being in" and "being with" the world of nature. The "becoming" aspect of nature play relates more to the future adults the children will become in relation to the natural environment (Beery, Chawla & Levin 2020).

Efforts to deepen young children's connectedness to nature require an understanding of and respect for both the "being" and "becoming" aspects of their relationship with nature. Rich sensory experiences, bodily movements, and self-directed explorations can contribute to both of these aspects, as they enrich a child's life in the moment and may "motivate children to continue to seek out nature as they grow" (Beery, Chawla & Levin 2020, p. 19).

Unfortunately, efforts focusing on children's "becoming" sometimes result in limited appreciation of the "being" aspects of childhood. With "being", the emphasis is on "who children are in the world" (Rouse & Hyde 2024, p. 11), while "becoming" focuses on what and who children should become in the future. Embracing a spiritual pedagogy in the early years can balance the "being" and "becoming" of a child's world. Enacting a spiritual pedagogy, as described by one early childhood educator, includes "stillness, self-expression, and exploration through nature, music, and the joy of just 'being' at the moment" (Rouse & Hyde 2024, p. 9). A spiritual pedagogy doesn't ignore the "becoming" aspects of child development. It, in fact, reflects a "double direction:" caring for each child as he or she is while caring for what each child may become (Rouse & Hyde 2024).

Children's "being and becoming" through interactions with the natural world means that nature needs to be more than a passive backdrop to their activities. Children need to manipulate natural materials, splash in the water, and dig in the dirt. They need to climb over logs, carry sticks and stones, and harvest fruits and vegetables. The "do not touch" approach will never satisfy their curiosity or stir their emotions.

Contact with animals can also enhance young children's connectedness to nature and different aspects of their spiritual development. Interacting with animals can deepen children's understanding about what animals need and how they live. By interacting with animals, children can discover commonalities between themselves and other living creatures. Such interactions can also promote empathy, ecological perspective taking, and an appreciation of animals as kin. These understandings and dispositions don't occur in the abstract. To appreciate animals as kin, children need to have close relationships with individual animals. To develop empathy and ecological perspective taking, they need opportunities to actually sense or physically experience the perceived emotions or feelings of another (Young, Khalil & Wharton 2018).

An interesting aspect of the "becoming" dimension of children's nature connectedness relates to the "becoming with" – or "co-becoming with" – our "companion species" (the other-than-human beings) on Planet Earth. "Becoming with" includes the idea of "living and dying together" (Persson, Andrée & Caiman 2024, p. 1259). "Becoming with" can also mean "being who you became with" as you experienced a close relationship with companion species (Haraway 2008). Children's interactions with different elements of nature indicate that they can "become with" not only companion species but also "stones, lichens, ice, birds, mosses, a mouse, a fire ball, and more indistinctly, patterns and landscapes" (Persson, Andrée & Caiman 2024, p. 1256).

Animism

"Becoming with" reflects a type of sensibility associated with animism (or "animistic sensibility"). Animism, which attributes sentience to other beings, allows us to see the world and all its different elements as "alive" and deserving of our respect (Persson, Andrée & Caiman 2024). Lynda Lynn Haupt (2021) identifies animism as one of the tenets of humans' rootedness with the rest of the natural world. These tenets, she says, "are grounded in millennia of human relations to the wild earth that have come to us across cultures through writings, art, science, and storytellings" (Haupt 2021, p. 23). In discussing animism, Haupt notes how there is no such thing as "mere" matter. "All ways of being, from hominid to dandelion to dragonfly to cedar tree possess a kind of aliveness" (p. 24).

Gregory Cajete (2001) – a Pueblo Native American and professor of American Indian Education and Native American Studies – describes animism as a basic human trait allowing humans to see the world as full of active entities. This way of seeing the world, he says, is consistent with the worldview held by most Indigenous people. The Western scientific view, on the other hand, tends to emphasize abstract concepts versus lived experiences. As Cajete (2001) notes, abstraction can lead to atrophy of our sensibilities and a type of blindness that denies the spirit and intelligence of the rest of the natural world.

Lisa Sideris (2017), in *Consecrating Science*, addresses some of the limitations and concerns about over-reliance on Western science as a way of knowing. She notes how the concepts we gain through the application of the scientific method provide only a fragmented view of the world. She also notes how some of the methods used in the pursuit of science reflect a moral or ethical deficiency. Isolating, abstracting, and objectifying are forms of manipulation and control which can lead to the dismantling of mystery and wonder.

Cajete (2001) proposes a different approach to learning about the natural world. He uses the term "native science" as "a metaphor for Native knowledge and creative participation with the natural world in both theory and practice" (p. 14). Native science, he says, is based on the understanding that "nature is not simply a collection of objects, but rather a dynamic, ever-flowing river of creation inseparable from our perceptions" (p. 15). He notes how the Western way of thinking, on the other hand, tends to categorically separate the animate from the inanimate elements of the Earth. The ethical implications of this way of thinking have been described as "environmentally devastating" (Bai 2015, p. 135). This way of thinking may also reflect and/or lead to a spiritual and moral void in our lives.

Relating to the more-than-human elements of the natural world as kin is vital for the health and well-being of children as well as for the natural environment (Giusti et al. 2018; Wilson 2022). Rejecting kinship and dismissing animistic ways of seeing and being in relationship with the rest of the natural world can lead to devastation of the human spirit as well as the natural world. Terry Tempest Williams (2008) says it well: "Our kinship with Earth must be maintained, otherwise, we will find ourselves trapped in the center of our own paved-over souls with no way out" (p. 75).

Nature as Play Partner

Nature, for the young child, is much more than a setting or resource to be used. Nature is something young children can interact with. As discussed in Chapter 3, affordances of the natural environment invite young children's active engagement. Children responding to these invitations enter into a type of partnership with the natural elements around them (Wilson 2022).

A team of researchers, after conducting a review of the literature on nature play during the early childhood years, concluded that "nature-based environments function as a play partner" (Prins et al. 2022, p. 13). They described ways in which the "living character of nature-based zones sparked curiosity and wonder, and invited play with critters and plants" (p. 10). Observations and conclusions drawn from this review of the literature – as well as from other research (Goodenough, Waite & Wright 2020; Kuh, Ponte & Chau, 2013) – indicate that children play differently in natural outdoor environments than they do indoors or on traditional outdoor playgrounds. This difference in play may be due to the affordances available to them and to the reciprocity that children experience while playing in natural environments.

Children may discover that a nature-rich environment has "a life of its own" with the ability to "play back" (Prins et al. 2022). Children in such environments often listen to and tune in to the invitations that such environments offer. The environment both instigates and enriches the children's play experiences. Nature as a play partner "affords not only play actions, but also play scripts" (Prins et al. 2022, p. 11). Some of these scripts impart spiritual messages to the children, including the message that they "are part of a **living** system" (Prins et al. 2022, p. 12).

Nature Play and Spiritual Development

The affordances of natural environments invite interaction. Many such affordances are in the form of loose parts (elements that can be manipulated, such as stones, leaves, sand, and sticks). These loose parts invite different types of play. Sticks and stones, for example, are often used for constructive and dramatic play, whether it involves just one child or a small group of children. In either case, imagination, exploration, and experimentation tend to be part of the process.

Deborah Schein describes how children at play with loose parts – especially loose parts found in nature – often experience moments of wonder, joy, awe, and peace. "It is during such moments that a child's spiritual development is being nurtured" (Schein 2018, p. 135). Schein's work includes the development of a Loose Parts Laboratory in Minneapolis, Minnesota. This project is modelled after Remida, a cultural project originating in Italy, which calls for a new look at things generally considered to be imperfect or useless. The project's focus is on sustainability, creativity, and research on what we call "waste materials." The Remida project challenges us to think differently about things that are often discarded or dismissed as being imperfect or useless.

Centres like Remida exist throughout the world. They're filled with recycled, reused, and repurposed items that, instead of being sent to garbage dumps, are put to educational and artistic use. Children using materials gathered from these centres are introduced to the idea of sustainability and care for the environment. They also learn to appreciate the way that different people express themselves in creative ways. Finally, children playing with loose parts experience the joy of creativity and come to a fuller appreciation of their own unique way of exploring their world. Such experiences support children as they continue their journey of "becoming" and "becoming with."

Schein's work (2018) includes research on the role of nature in promoting child development, especially in relation to spirituality. Her work supports the understanding that "the relationship between nature and spiritual development runs deep" (p. 82). Schein's work also highlights three types of spiritual sensitivity as identified by Hay and Nye (2006): awareness-sensing, mystery-sensing, and value-sensing.

Awareness-sensing involves being alert or paying attention to spiritual matters. This occurs within self-awareness, along with an evolving understanding of the natural world and one's place in this world. Mystery-sensing involves an awareness of the unknown. This occurs "when children have opportunities to use their imaginations while exploring and being in moments of wonder, wonderment, awe, joy, or inner peace" (Schein 2018, p. 83). "Value-sensing" focuses on "feelings and emotions more than cognition…. It implies … that cognition must build on a child's emotional and spiritual state" (Schein 2018, p. 85).

Sensory and Whole-Body Experiences

The development of spiritual sensitivity depends, in part, on what we experience through our bodily senses, including our sense of self-movement (proprioception). As human beings, we are always bodily in the world. Our bodies and senses are in constant interaction with our surroundings. The content of these surroundings and our related interactions shape our inner and outer landscapes. This is especially true for young children.

What children experience through their bodily senses plays a pivotal role in the way they come to know the world. It also plays a role in the attachment process, including their attachment to nature (Christian 2020). Children's attachment to nature is nurtured through sensory perceptions, not abstract analysis. For nature to be more than an abstraction, children need to experience it with full body engagement.

Bodily engagement with nature can help children develop what has been referred to as "haptic rapport" (Kline 2023). "Haptic" relates to the sense of touch, especially in relation to the perception and manipulation of objects. "Rapport" generally suggests a feeling of familiarity, comfortableness, and friendliness. Haptic rapport may play a necessary role in children's attachment to nature.

"Haptic rapport" includes the "intimacies and meaning-making" associated with human engagement with the more-than-human physical world. This engagement includes both movement and sensory experiences. It also involves an exchange of information between humans and the more-than-human world (Kline 2023).

Developing haptic rapport with the more-than-human world requires numerous opportunities to touch and feel the various elements of the natural world, such as soil, water, wind, and the warmth of the sun. These physical sensations serve as pathways connecting mind, body, and the more-than-human world. These sensations also allow for exchanges, or reciprocity, between self and the world outside of self. In other words, the sensory and tactile experiences we have with the more-than-human world "do not stop at the skin"; they connect mind and body, internal and external worlds. Haptic rapport allows children to "sense communion and feel belonging through their touch-based relationships with more-than-human natures" (Kline 2023, p. 2).

The importance of children's sensory engagement with nature was highlighted in a study that analysed children's experience with nature in four dimensions: sensory, affective, cognitive, and behavioural (Linzmayer, Halpenny & Walker 2014). Findings of this study suggest that the senses may be a primary, foundational component of children's experiences with nature and that sensory engagement is the underlying link between contact with nature and children's affective states. While cognition and behaviour also emerged as important dimensions of children's experiences with nature, they seemed to be secondary to the sensory and affective dimensions.

Other research – including a review of the literature (van Heel, van den Born & Aarts 2023) – documents the importance of sensory engagement for fostering children's connections to nature. This review included 122 articles published between 2001 and 2021. Different dimensions of connectedness with nature – from physical to spiritual – were addressed. The most frequently specified dimensions of connectedness with nature were emotional or affective. Overall findings of this review indicate that the most effective ways to strengthen young children's connectedness to nature include (1) providing opportunities for self-directed explorations in sensory nature-rich environments and (2) engaging them in thoughtful reflections on their relationship with nature (van Heel, van den Born & Aarts 2023). The self-directed explorations necessarily involve bodily movement, engagement of the senses, and meaning-making.

False dualisms about the way we view ourselves and the world around us can lead to limiting our practices while working with children. Making a distinction between the mind and body, for example, may cause us to overlook ways in which the soma or body plays in emotion, thought, and action. "Soma", which might be translated from the Greek as "body", has evolved to mean "the body living in its wholeness." This concept highlights how our physical sensations and movements can impact not only our emotions and mental well-being but also our way of knowing ourselves and the world around us.

The body and movements of the body are highly influential in shaping our perception, learning, and knowledge. They are also highly influential in shaping and enhancing our appreciation of the natural world. Children need bodily (sensory and movement) experiences with nature in order to establish a relationship with it. They need experiences that engage their emotions, senses, and actions, not just their thoughts. The same is true for supporting the spiritual dimensions of connectedness to nature. The spiritual dimensions aren't abstractions. They're realities experienced through and by the body but known by one's entire being: body, mind, and spirit.

A 2025 study found that children, after embodied interactions with nature (e.g., "making snowman," "wrapping arms around tree," "talking to chickens"), reported a greater sense of presence in nature than children whose interactions relied solely on vision (e.g., "seeing snow," "seeing moss," "watching pileated woodpecker"). "Presence" was described as a "state of heightened awareness and connection" which included "being highly aware without thought … and/or feeling connected to something beyond the self" (Gray et al. 2025, p. 3).

Conclusion

Nature play means more than playing in nature; it involves playing *with* nature. In nature play, the natural environment provides more than a setting and materials for play. Nature becomes a partner in the process. Nature play makes important contributions to the development of the whole child, including spiritual development.

> **BOX 8.2   SUGGESTIONS: SUPPORTING SPIRITUAL DEVELOPMENT**
>
> Each chapter in Deborah Schein's book, *Inspiring Wonder, Awe, and Empathy*, includes ideas for what parents and teachers can do to support young children's spiritual development. The following ten implications for practice are based on her suggestions offered in this book and elsewhere (Wilson & Schein 2017). Each of these suggestions can be implemented during children's nature play activities.
>
> 1. Promote authentic relationships between children and objects, children and nature, children and educators, and children and family members. Authentic relationships go beyond use or what is practical. Authentic relationships are based on respect and care.
> 2. Focus more on self-awareness than self-esteem. "Self-awareness focuses on helping children learn about themselves in relationship to all that exists around them" (Schein 2018, p. 28). Self-awareness places the child in a social versus individualistic setting.
> 3. Honor children's emotions. When a child is joyful, celebrate the joyful moment with the child. When a child is sad or hurt, show understanding and support.
> 4. View children's questions as windows into their spiritual ways of thinking. Wonder with them about the mysteries of life.
> 5. Provide opportunities for children to be alone and reflective. Meaning-making requires personal reflection.
> 6. Use recyclables or loose parts for creative activities. The open-endedness of these materials invites

creativity. The use of recyclables also promotes a sustainability mindset.
7. Acknowledge children's acts of kindness, empathy, and reverence.
8. Invite children to listen to their own breath, to the world of nature, and to each other.
9. Create a welcoming, beautiful, inviting, and stimulating environment.
10. Recognize and honour the uniqueness of each individual child.

9

Mindfulness in Nature

Mindfulness

"We sit together, the mountain and me, until only the mountain remains." These two lines from a poem by Chinese poet Li Po (700–762) express a sense of oneness between himself and the other-than-human world. Other lines in this mindfulness poem reflect the poet's close observation of what he sees and experiences in the moment. He sees the birds vanishing and the clouds draining away. Eventually, his sense of self is gone, as well – "only the mountain remains." This poem, "Zazen on Ching-t'ing Mountain", offers no judgement or explanation of what is seen or experienced. There's simply an awareness of the moment and a de-centring of the self. That's basically what mindfulness is all about.

We sometimes call mindfulness a practice, but it's also a gift. Mindfulness enriches our experience of being alive. We tend to live distracted versus mindful lives. For most of us, this distracted way of living is so entrenched that we don't even notice that our attention has been hijacked. We may be so caught up in messages from the ever-present media and in thoughts about what we need or want or feel we have to do that we can no longer be mindful of the present moment. These distractions can soon erode our quality of life.

Mindfulness, as a gift, can help us return to a more meaningful, joyful, and fulfilling experience of life. It can lead us away from the automaticity of the distracted life (Thiermann & Sheate 2021). Mindfulness as a practice reminds us to attend to what really matters. It helps us focus on the moment and puts us in touch with the "suchness" of what we are experiencing. "Suchness denotes the undifferentiated wholeness of reality, in its vivid originality. According to Buddhist thought, suchness is the world as it is, in its own vivacity and wholeness" (Chang 2020, p. 6). Li Po experienced "suchness" in his sense of being one with the mountain. He wasn't studying or analysing the mountain. He was simply being present to and with it.

Mindfulness as a practice involves the self-regulation of attention and a particular orientation towards one's experiences in the present moment (Barrable et al. 2021). Self-regulation keeps us focused on the immediate experience versus expending thought and energy on the past or future. Having a particular focus or orientation involves curiosity, openness, and acceptance. This orientation can generate new understandings about the world around you.

BOX 9.1 RESEARCH NOTE: MINDFULNESS AND CONNECTEDNESS TO NATURE

A mindfulness study conducted by Barrable et al. (2021) involved young children in three different nature-related activities: mindful listening to the sounds of nature, mindful looking at nature near and far, and pretending to be animals. These three activities were chosen based on what are generally understood to be components of mindfulness: (a) self-regulation of attention and (b) an orientation characterized by curiosity, openness, and acceptance. This study was based on the understanding that contact with nature alone may not be enough to enhance connectedness to nature – that the type or quality of the nature contact could also matter. The specific question addressed in this study related to whether or not adding mindfulness to nature contact would increase the children's connectedness to nature.

Assessments conducted with 74 children before and after they participated in the three mindfulness activities at a nature reserve showed an increase in both nature connectedness and positive affect (feeling more lively and joyful). These results are consistent with other research showing that mindfulness in nature may foster a sense of oneness and enhance one's connectedness with nature (Unsworth, Palicki & Lustig 2016).

Reference

Barrable, A., Booth, D., Adams, D. & Beachamp, G. (2021). Enhancing nature connection and positive affect in children through mindful engagement with natural environments. *International Journal of Environmental Research and Public Health*, 18(9), 4785.

Mindfulness in Nature

Being in and with nature may be one of the most powerful ways to enter a place of mindfulness (Van Gordon, Shonin & Richardson 2018). Nature-based mindfulness may also be qualitatively different than mindfulness in non-natural settings (Djernis et al. 2019). Practicing mindfulness in nature allows us to be completely present and engaged with the natural environment around us. It's about noticing the sights, sounds, and other sensory stimuli of what we're experiencing in nature at that very moment. This isn't about "studying" nature to increase our knowledge about nature, nor is it about analysing our feelings about nature. As noted in the poem by Li Po, mindfulness in nature is about decentring the self and entering a place of oneness with nature.

Practicing mindfulness in nature means more than just going outside and experiencing the natural world. It's about cultivating awareness of what we're experiencing. Rachel Carson (1956), in *The Sense of Wonder*, notes how hearing the sounds of nature can be a source of great pleasure, but "it requires conscious cultivation" (p. 68). She explains how some people had never heard the song of certain birds even though those birds are in their backyards every spring. She urges us to "Take time to listen and talk about the voices of the earth and what they mean – the majestic voice of thunder, the winds, the sound of surf or flowing streams" (p. 68). In listening to the dawn chorus of birds, she says, "one hears the throb of life itself" (p. 69). This is, indeed, a spiritual experience.

Children and Mindfulness in Nature

One of the goals of mindfulness in nature for young children, as discussed by Deb Schein (2018), is to "achieve an acute awareness of the world and one's own place in it" (p. 75). Such awareness can foster deeper nature connectedness or self-nature interconnectedness (Unsworth, Palicki & Lustig 2016).

Spending time in nature can take many forms and provide a variety of benefits. Perhaps the most effective way to experience the spirituality and personal well-being benefits of time in nature is to combine nature engagement with intentional mindful awareness. At times, such mindful awareness generates intense feelings of awe and wonder. Such feelings tend to run deeper than aesthetic appreciation. Jeff Thompson, in an article published in *Frontiers in Psychology*, provides a personal example of this. Thompson (2022) describes how he, a city dweller, once hiked alone to the top of a mountain and, after reaching the summit, intentionally took in the panoramic view all around him. He felt, at that moment, something pass through his entire body – "not just on my skin: it was much deeper.... I realized then that this must be awe" (pp. 3–4). Awe – though often a momentary feeling – is associated with enhanced learning, creativity, humility, gratitude, optimism, openness, and critical thinking (Thompson 2022).

While most of the research on mindfulness in nature focuses on adults, some studies looked specifically at children. A 2023 review of the literature focusing on the impacts of nature connectedness on children's well-being included 72 studies, most of them considering children's psychological well-being. The benefits of nature connectedness identified through this review included experiences of mindfulness or spirituality (Arola et al. 2023). In another study, children were asked to share their views of nature and to describe their experiences in nature. Some children, including children as young as six or seven, reported feeling a sense of oneness with nature (Moula, Walshe & Lee 2023).

Witnessing young children engaged in mindfulness in nature isn't unusual. It's something they seem programmed to do. Young children have active, curious minds and are drawn to novelty or newness. The following story about Kevin and the moss provides an example of this.

Kevin, a four-year-old at a preschool in New Mexico, discovered some moss growing at the base of a tree in the playyard. Moss growing there was somewhat unusual, due to the dry conditions of the desert environment. Kevin spent a considerable amount of time looking at the moss and feeling it. He gathered some stones and used them to surround the small patch of moss. One day, after he had been absent for about a week, Kevin discovered that the moss was brown and almost brittle. He seemed curious and concerned. Was the moss dying? Kevin asked for a sprinkling can and some water. He wanted to give the moss a drink to help it "get better." The next day, he was delighted to see the moss turning green again.

This story about Kevin and the moss is a mindfulness story. After noticing something new (the moss), Kevin spent time being with it and observing it. His mind and heart became engaged, with the moss being the focus of his attention. When the moss seemed to be dying, Kevin worked to save it. We see in this story a pairing of mindfulness and caring about nature. Kevin displays empathy, curiosity, creativity, and problem-solving. He reaches outside of himself to care for another living thing. This "reaching out" nurtures not only the moss but his own biophilia as well. The caring aspect of "reaching out" is critical to a more harmonious human–nature relationship. It is also a contributor to holistic human development for individuals and for communities (Smith et al. 2025).

Caring for nature, if supported during the early childhood years, can extend throughout adulthood (Chawla 2007) with benefits to humans and the environment. One way to promote such caring involves broadening the focus of early childhood environmental education to include a sustainability focus. As already indicated, early childhood education for sustainability doesn't mean telling young children that they need to "save the Earth." It's about inviting them to reflect on and respond to their relationship with the more-than-human world. This concept is "grounded in an understanding of inter-connectedness and an ethic of partnership with all of nature" (Wilson 2020, p. 16). It is also grounded in an understanding of reciprocity (Wang 2017). These understandings can be strengthened through mindfulness in nature.

Encouraging children to care for the natural world should be an integral part of nature play, not an alternative or add-on. Doing so adds depth and an element of "mindful learning" to efforts in connecting children with nature (Deringer 2017). Mindfulness as a key component of a pedagogy for sustainable development at the early childhood level is supported by the academic literature (Barrable 2019).

Environments Promoting Mindfulness

Not all environments are of equal value in supporting mindfulness. Generally, children are more likely to engage in mindfulness activities in natural environments than built environments. The sensory stimuli of natural environments draw attention to what is being experienced in the present moment – the sound of wind in the trees, the sight of migrating or nesting birds, the taste of ripe strawberries, and the feel of warm sand. Attention to such sensory stimuli is effortless and is sometimes described as being "restorative" (Nguyen & Walters 2024). Related benefits for young children include a sense of calmness and relaxation. Effortless attention to the sensory stimuli of a nature-rich environment can also lead to slower and more concentrated play (Nedovic & Morrissey 2013), which often includes elements of spirituality (Mata-McMahon 2019).

Nature-rich environments provide both passive and active stimuli. Just being present in a nature-rich area provides passive stimulation through the feeling of "being away" (Izenstark & Ebata 2019). This feeling can be a pleasant distraction from some of the anxieties and concerns that young children might be carrying around with them. For example, a young child, new to a nature preschool, may have some anxieties about being separated from her parents. A bird at a birdbath may distract her from this concern.

This "being away" factor may be especially important for children who have experienced adverse conditions such as poverty, abuse, and neglect or have experienced other forms of trauma in their lives. Research indicates that exposure to nature can help children cope with adversity and that different forms of nature engagement can reduce stress and anxiety (Chatterjee 2018; Fisher 2022). Research also indicates that nature may serve as a protective factor before the harmful impacts of adversity occur (Touloumakos & Barrable 2020).

The dynamic sensory elements of nature-rich environments can also work as active stimuli, inviting children to become bodily engaged with natural phenomena such as water flowing in a stream. "Both the active engagement and the passive stimulus are believed to have an effect on mindfulness" (Sahni & Kumar 2021, p. 458).

Certain aspects of the social environment can also hinder or facilitate mindfulness in nature. Alone time can be a facilitator. We sometimes think of young children's solitary play as less mature and less complex than other forms of play. This view can, at times, be misleading. A child involved in solitary play may actually be engaged in mindfulness. Solitary play, in such instances, can include contemplation or thoughtful observation. This form of solitary play can be both a reflection of and a path to deeper connectedness with nature (Beery & Lekies 2019).

A related study found that children who spent more time in nature scored higher on a connectedness-to-nature scale than children who do not. While this was to be expected, findings also showed that what children did while in nature made a difference. The most important predictor of high connectedness to nature was spending time alone in nature. Children who spent outside time alone in nature weekly were almost 35% more likely to have high connectedness-to-nature scores than those spending time outside alone less frequently (Szczytko et al. 2020). Actually spending alone time in nature may not be especially applicable to preschool children. Yet understanding that solitary play may contribute to mindfulness should be considered.

Suggestions for Fostering Mindfulness in Nature

Watch young children in a nature-rich environment and you'll see that they readily engage in a type of mindfulness without any prompting from adults. Yet there are ways we can support the process and possibly enhance the spiritual benefits of mindfulness in nature.

Integrate Mindfulness and Place-Based Education

Mindfulness in nature can be fostered by integrating it into place-based education, which is defined as a dynamic learning process in the context of the local community (Deringer 2017). Place-based education focuses on the relationship between people and the rest of the natural environment within that community. Mindfulness practices can strengthen place-based education by encouraging students and teachers to be more attentive to their local environments and aware of related environmental and social justice concerns. Mindfulness when integrated into place-based education can help students view their communities with greater sensitivity and openness to new insights and information.

Slow Things Down

Perhaps one of the best ways to encourage children's mindfulness in nature is to slow things down. This approach to working with children – sometimes referred to as "slow pedagogy" (Chang 2020) – is more consistent with the rhythms of nature and the way young children learn than the fast pedagogies often emphasized in educational programs. Fast pedagogies value efficiency in the teaching-learning process and are based on accountability or standards specifying what students should know and be able to do at certain junctures in their educational journeys. Slow pedagogy is based on a different philosophy, which allows learning to unfold in its own natural rhythm. Learning achieved through slow pedagogy tends to be deeper and more satisfying than learning achieved through fast pedagogy.

Slow pedagogy values personal reflection and meaning-making. Reflection, in this context, refers to giving serious thought to something. What one reflects on may be an object, a happening, an idea, or even one's feelings. Reflection might take the form of a question: What's going on here? What am I witnessing? What's the meaning of this? Reflecting on experience "is a significant factor in spiritual development" (Wills 2025, p. 10). While reflection and meaning-making are aspects of learning that are challenging to measure or to fit into a specific timeframe, they play important roles in a child's holistic development.

Slow pedagogy, as applied to environmental education, might be called "eco-pedagogy" – a form of pedagogy allowing students "to pause or dwell in spaces for more than a fleeting moment" (Payne & Wattchow 2009, p. 16). Slow pedagogy is in tune with what Claire Warden (2015) refers to as "nature time." This form of pedagogy gives children the opportunity to attach meaning to, and receive meaning from, the environment they're in. The children not only learn *in* the natural environment but also *from* and *with* that environment.

For many of us, the culture in which we live is based on "fast knowledge" (Orr 1994). This type of knowledge, which is easily accessed through the internet, is divorced from its ecological and social context. "Fast knowledge", while more efficient than "slow knowledge", lacks depth and is rarely sufficient for guiding meaningful action. To really understand our place within the larger ecological system, we need to embrace slow knowledge. Slowing things down while working with young children gives them the chance to experience and appreciate the kind of knowing that comes with patient attentiveness.

Encourage Savouring the Beauty of Nature

Mindfulness helps us tune in to the sensory-rich features of the natural environment and allows us to experience the joy and satisfaction of a savouring moment. As discussed in earlier chapters, savouring the beauty of nature leads to appreciation and respect, which, in turn, can lead to care and saving.

One simple exercise to promote mindful engagement of beauty involves asking children to identify three good things in nature. Research assessing the impact of this simple practice found that people identifying "three good things in nature" each day over a period of five consecutive days gained significantly deeper nature connectedness and improved psychological health (Richardson & Sheffield 2017).

Another idea for tuning in to the beauty of nature is to invite each child to identify and spend time in a special "sit spot", which is simply a favourite place in nature to visit regularly. The idea of a "sit spot" is to cultivate awareness by tuning in to sensory stimuli and noticing details and patterns of the immediate natural surroundings.

Promote "Contemplative Wonder" and "Spiritual Awe"

"Contemplative wonder" differs from some other forms of wonder, especially the kind of wonder that engages the mind more than the heart. Wonder as a cognitive process involves thinking and/or questioning. Examples are wondering if the rain will stop by early afternoon or if putting all the books in one box will make it too heavy to carry. Wondering as a cognitive process might also involve thoughtful consideration about something. We sometimes refer to this form of wonder as "pondering." We might, for example, ponder the merits of a change in the daily routine to see if that might be more engaging for the children. Young children might engage in this form of wondering as they try to figure out how to construct a shelter in the woods.

Wonder as a manifestation of spirituality is "so much more than pondering" (Robinson 2022). "Contemplative wonder" engages the heart more than the mind. It's more about experiencing mystery than looking for answers. While some forms of wonder (or pondering) might focus on scientific questions, "contemplative wonder" tends to focus on existential questions and meaning making. "Contemplative wonder" is fuelled by the imagination and is often experienced as fascination, joy, transcendence, and delight.

Typical discourses of wonder often used in the environmental education literature generally fail to acknowledge "contemplative wonder" (Chang 2020). Typical discourses tend to reflect a "western tradition in which nature is seen aglow" and the wilderness as "a place of excitement and enchantment" (Chang 2020, p. 2). Viewing the outdoors as a place of wonder in this sense can imply a certain bias and reinforce a partial notion of the natural world. It may also neglect a great variety of nature-related experiences, including the experience of contemplative wonder and spiritual awe (Chang 2020).

Practices promoting contemplative wonder and spiritual awe tap into some of the more subtle aspects of nature. Such practices can open the door to encounters with the "suchness" and mystery of nature which may otherwise go unnoticed. "Contemplative practice aims for nothing more than attention to the present … a clear awareness of the wild" (Chang 2020, p. 8). Listening deeply to the elements of nature is one such contemplative practice. One elementary student who listens intently to plants once explained how "listening deeply to the elements" differs from "thinking about the elements." "If you're thinking then you're not really listening." When asked if she really *hears* the plants, she responded by saying, "Yeah, but you have to hear it through your heart" (Piersol 2015, p. 134).

Promoting deep listening and contemplative wonder during outdoor activities requires a shift from the usual educational approach which tends to *pursue* experiences of wonder "to readying our minds and bodies to *receive* [italics added] the wonder that is already there" (Chang 2020, p. 10). "Readying our minds" involves dropping our pre-conceived ideas or expectations of wonder and "inviting the natural world to show us what wonder is" (Chang 2020, p. 10). Contemplative wonder – as a characteristic of spirituality – engages the whole body and allows the child to become engaged with the many wonder-full aspects of the natural world (Robinson 2022).

Integrate Yoga and other Contemplative Practices while Working with Young Children

Simple yoga can be done with young children to promote both mindfulness and nature connectedness. Doing poses akin to such things as trees and birds can encourage closer observation and stronger affinity to the world of nature. For a tree pose, children can be asked to stand tall like a tree, stretch out their arms like branches, and perhaps sway a bit in response to the wind. Children can also be invited to feel the sun on their leaves and to draw water up through their roots. For a bird pose, children can be asked to open and close their wings or sit quietly in their nest. With a bit of encouragement, children will come up with many other ideas of yoga poses inspired by animals and other elements of the natural world.

Walking a labyrinth is another contemplative practice that can be done with young children. A labyrinth is a simple, circular pattern, usually laid out on the ground, intended for walking with mindfulness. The circular path takes the walker to the centre of the pattern and back out again. There are no wrong turns or dead ends. Walking a labyrinth can help children feel calm and peaceful. Before walking a labyrinth, children will need some guidance on how do so respectfully. Involving the children in making a labyrinth can also be a contemplative experience.

Other contemplative practices shared by early childhood teachers include morning stretches, special songs, simple breathing exercises, and guided meditations (Mata-McMahon 2019; Mata-McMahon, Haslip & Schein 2020).

Prepare the Environment for Mindfulness

Invitations to mindfulness can come from the environment as well as from human adults. While almost anything in a natural environment can invite close observation and mindfulness, certain features may be especially helpful. Well-placed gazing globes can call attention to intriguing aspects of the environment. A child-sized chair or bench next to a gazing globe may invite a child to sit awhile and really notice what is reflected in the globe: the beauty of clouds in the sky, the tree branches overhead, or a butterfly on the flowering bushes nearby. Secluded places in the yard can also invite silent retreat and mindful contemplation.

Amy Wagenfeld and Chad Kennedy (2024) refer to places of retreat as "cozy places." They note how children may need time to take a break from more active play or to acclimate themselves to the play space and people in the space. They note, too, how cozy places can help children self-regulate, a necessary skill for regulating one's behaviour and emotions. The sense of calm and safety that children may experience in a cozy place may also invite reflection about the world around them. Wagenfeld and Kennedy – both landscape designers with extensive experience in therapeutic design for children – indicate that cozy places should offer good visibility of the surroundings with some texture on surfaces to create tactile interest. A cozy place may be under a deck or ramp, in a small crawl-in den, or under a tree with low-hanging branches.

Help Children Reflect on Their Experiences in and with Nature

Learning environments and nature-based activities are often planned around children's interests and/or specific desired outcomes. Digging up carrots or filling a birdbath are examples of activities that most children enjoy. We can extend the enjoyment and meaning of such activities by inviting children to reflect on the experience. A reflection can be in the form of a conversation about what the children did and how they felt during the activity. Conversation starters might be in the form of questions: What are you seeing? How does this make you feel? Questions might also relate to what was observed in the natural environment: Do you think that bird was looking at us?

Reflection can also be fostered by asking children to represent an activity, observation, or insight through a drawing or other form of creative expression. Another idea is to have the children dictate and illustrate a story about their experiences. This story, when shared with parents or other caregivers, gives children yet another opportunity to reflect on and find meaning in what they did and experienced.

Modelling reflection can also be helpful. You can model reflection by sharing some of your observations, feelings, and thoughts. You might say something like "Watching the ducks on the pond makes me feel peaceful" or "I'm wondering how that tree can grow in such a rocky place."

> **BOX 9.2 REFLECTIONS: RHYTHM**
>
> When we think of rhythm, we often think of music; but other aspects of life have rhythm, as well. There's generally a rhythm to our day, to the way we walk and talk, to the way we eat and breathe, even to the beating of our heart. We also see rhythm in the different aspects of the natural world – the changing seasons, the oceans' tides, the migration of birds and butterflies. Helping children become more aware of nature's rhythms can foster their sense of wonder and their interest in the natural world.
>
> In music, rhythm refers to the interplay between sounds and silences. It's rhythm that gives structure to the composition and makes the music come alive. Early childhood educators know that young children have rhythm, as well. Adults working with young children know that things go better when the pace and structure of the day match the needs and interests of the children. The pace may be fast at times – as when a child enthusiastically rolls down a hill. But it can also be slow, as when a child carefully arranges leaves and petals to create a work of art.
>
> Stillness and silence can add a special dimension to the rhythm of the day. A child, watching a rabbit chew a blade of grass, may stand completely still for an extended period of time. This moment of being wrapped (rapt) in wonder may be just as important to the child as the silence is to the pause between notes in a musical composition.

Conclusion

Mindfulness in nature can promote deeper connectedness to nature and enhance the spiritual development of young children. Even young children can benefit from contemplative practices such as yoga, walking a labyrinth, meditation, and solitary time in a "sit spot." These and other mindfulness practices in nature can help children gain a sense of being one with, versus separate from, nature.

10

Philosophical Thinking

The Need to Nurture Biophilia

Biophilia was defined in Chapter 1 as the "tendency to affiliate with life and lifelike processes" (Wilson 2006). Chapter 1 also issued a warning about how our biophilic values can atrophy (Kellert 2012). Biophilia may be with us from birth, but without nourishment, it can diminish over time. Rachel Carson (1956) addressed this concern in *The Sense of Wonder*. She first describes how children experience the world as "fresh and new and beautiful" and then notes how, for most of us, "that true instinct for what is beautiful and awe-inspiring, is dimmed and even lost before we reach adulthood" (p. 42).

Kellert (2012) refers to biophilia as a "birthright" yet recognizes the fact that it is "not a hard-wired outcome." The flourishing of biophilia, he says, requires a "conscious and sustained engagement" with nature (p. xiii). Kellert explains how modern society's tendency to consider nature "a dispensable amenity rather than a necessity for health and happiness" generates environmental and social problems. What's needed, he says, is a "new consciousness and ethic toward nature" (p. xiv). Nurturing biophilia during the early years is one way to promote this new consciousness.

Ecological Consciousness

Important distinctions are sometimes made between "ecological consciousness" and "environmental consciousness." Ecological consciousness includes a spiritual component which may or may not be part of environmental consciousness. Ecological consciousness recognizes the sacredness and sentience of life. This form of consciousness is grounded in an eco-centric orientation which has been described as "a deep awareness of one's biological, ecological, affective, and spiritual connection to nonhuman nature" (White 2011, p. 42).

Environmental consciousness, on the other hand, tends to have a human-focused orientation. It includes an awareness of how human actions impact the environment. Environmental consciousness allows for a sense of self as separate from the rest of the natural world. With ecological consciousness, the human focus steps aside, making room for a "vaster inner beingness to arise" (White 2011, p. 43). Ecological consciousness recognizes the interconnectedness between self and the rest of nature or "self-in-kinship" with nature (White 2011, p. 45). Engaging children in philosophical thinking is one way to promote ecological consciousness.

Philosophical Thinking

In today's world, how we, as humans, use the land isolates many of us from regular interaction with the natural world. Thus, we are no longer having the same number or types of nature-related experiences as our ancestors did. Some refer to this diminished interaction with nature as "extinction of experience" (Richardson et al. 2022; Soga & Gaston 2016; Pyle 1993).

Diminished opportunity to interact with nature, however, is only one of the major contributors to "extinction of experience." Loss of orientation towards nature is another major factor (Colléony, Cohen-Seffer & Shwartz 2020; Richardson et al. 2022). "Orientation," in this context, refers to people's desire to be in nature (Chang et al. 2022) and/or the way in which people "emotionally connect with nature and commit to protect the natural world" (Colléony, Cohen-Seffer & Shwartz 2020, p. 2).

Human connections with nature are both externally and internally defined. Externally defined connections are based on material and experiential experiences. Internally defined connections are more cognitive, emotional, and philosophical. While both the "internal" and "external" components of connections with nature play important roles in sustainability efforts, the "internal" components may be more critical in creating the kind of system change required for a sustainable future. Philosophical thinking is proposed as one avenue for strengthening the internally defined connections (Ives et al. 2018).

While philosophy, for many people, may be an intimidating subject, it boils down to a search for meaning and understanding. Philosophy asks thought-provoking questions: What makes something "good" or "right"? Why do people and pets die? What does it mean to really love someone or something? Asking such questions helps us develop a healthy outlook on life. Philosophical questioning also plays a role in individual and collective identity formation (Templeton & Eccles 2006).

Children and Philosophical Thinking

Engaging children in philosophical thinking about nature and their relationship with nature is one way to promote orientation towards and connections with nature. But are young children ready for philosophical thinking? The answer is "yes." Young children are not only ready for philosophical thinking, they're already doing it. We see this in young children's propensity for wonder, guessing, speculating, inferring, questioning, and developing ideas and beliefs (Matthews 1994). Young children are natural philosophers. "They approach philosophical topics with great minds that are uncluttered by the baggage that can accumulate as one gets older" (McCarty 2006, p. xi).

Philosophy is about ideas, and even young children demonstrate the ability to have unique and wonderful ideas. As Eleanor

Duckworth (2006) explains in *The Having of Wonderful Ideas*, children not only have philosophical ideas, they're also capable of testing those ideas.

Philosophical thinking – or philosophizing – is about wondering, imagining, and exploring. We know kids are good at that, but they sometimes need adult support or guidance to sharpen their focus. As philosophical thinking usually requires a certain amount of attentiveness and calmness, "cozy places" and "sit spots" in natural settings may be helpful. Other supports for philosophical thinking include unhurried time, music, art, poetry, and literature.

BOX 10.1   REFLECTIONS: *PLATO, NOT PROZAC!*

I was discussing the idea of philosophical thinking with a class of undergraduate students in early childhood education when I told them about a book I had read. I explained how the book, *Plato, Not Prozac!* (Marinoff 2000), suggests turning to philosophy versus drugs in our efforts to solve everyday problems. Some of the students thought I said "playdough" instead of "Plato." After some laughs, we talked about how working with playdough can, at times, provide opportunities for young children to gain insights about themselves and the world around them. We also identified ways in which philosophical thinking can be integrated into the daily activities of an early childhood classroom.

Playing with playdough engages the child's imagination and can lead to interesting insights. Playdough – as an open-ended material – allows for exploration and experimentation. As children use playdough, they experiment with ideas, not just materials. Children may start with a mental plan or picture of what they'd like to make. As they work, however, it's not unusual for additional ideas to emerge. A child using playdough to make an earthworm, for example, may begin to think about where earthworms live. They may try to make an underground home for the worms. The philosophical thinking behind this scenario may expand the child's focus beyond an isolated entity (the worm) to how it's connected to the larger world. Philosophical thinking often involves making connections versus considering individual things in isolation.

Philosophy with young children isn't about adding a new curricular area to the work we do with young children. It's about expanding the thinking and pondering the meaning behind what we already do. It's also about supporting children in the meaning-making process.

Philosophy and Ecological Perspective Taking

Philosophical thinking – in addition to the many benefits it offers individual children – can lead to benefits for the environment. These benefits relate to ecological perspective taking and pro-environmental behaviours. Perspective taking (understanding how a situation appears to someone else) is recognized as a critical part of child development. Ecological perspective taking (taking the perspective of plants, animals, or other natural elements) is a foundational step in developing a sense of respect and caring for the natural world.

Thinking critically about environmental issues can foster ecological perspective taking (Hedefalk, Almqvist & Ostman 2015) and is a central part of education for sustainable development (ESD). At one time, ESD with children focused on teaching facts about the environment and telling them what they should and should not do to protect the environment. This approach has proven to be largely ineffective. A more effective approach engages children in environmental problem-solving and meaningful collaboration in making decisions about the environment. This approach helps children consider a range of perspectives and think through what they themselves believe about the environment (Chawla & Cushing 2007).

Even at the preschool level, educators can help children consider issues that impact society and the environment.

Considering such issues often involves philosophical as well as scientific thinking. Asking questions about what worms eat and why we see more worms after it rains reflects scientific thinking. Such questions should be encouraged, but philosophical questions should also be considered. Children may ask, for example, if it's okay to use worms as bait when fishing. Avoiding a simple "yes" or "no" answer and engaging children in a discussion about this issue give children the opportunity to form some of their own beliefs. It also gives them an opportunity to engage in ecological perspective taking.

"I wonder …" statements can also be used with young children to support philosophical thinking and ecological perspective taking. For example, if children have been observing baby birds in a nearby nest, a statement like "I wonder if baby birds are anxious or fearful when their mother leaves the nest to look for food" can help children consider the needs or feelings of the birds. Another way to promote ecological perspective taking is to encourage children to pretend that they are other-than-human living things. Children will often do this spontaneously in their "pretend play" activities, but related props – such as costumes and nesting materials – can be helpful.

There are many examples in the literature of young children pretending to be animals. Such behaviours, when viewed through a spiritual lens, reflect a crossing of boundaries. As children become an animal, they enter what Jane Bone (2008) describes as a "spiritual elsewhere." Crossing of boundaries, she says, allows children to experience moments of "spiritual withness". "These are moments when it is possible to lose and find oneself at the same time in relationship with someone or something. Spiritual withness is a moment of intersubjectivity felt as an intense awareness of self and Other" (Bone 2008, p. 18).

An incident of children from Australia pretending to be kangaroos provides an example of how young children readily identify with animals in their surroundings. At first, the children showed a strong interest in getting a close-up look at kangaroos in the grasslands near their preschool. Over time, they displayed increasing confidence in getting closer and closer to the kangaroos. The kangaroos, in turn, seemed to become increasingly comfortable with the children's presence. They gradually allowed the children who approached slowly and quietly to get quite close.

With increased observation, the children began to notice differences between themselves and the kangaroos in modes of attention and behaviours. They noticed, for example, the kangaroos' large upright ears and the way the ears can swivel. They noticed, too, the kangaroos' enormous tails and how they use their tails to balance and jump. Some of the children wondered what it would be like to have a kangaroo's body. They made big tails, attached them to their own bodies, and then hopped around. They put their hands on their heads to mimic the action of protruding swivelling ears. After observing the carcass of a dead kangaroo, some of the children even pretended to be dead and dying kangaroos (Taylor & Pacini-Ketchabaw 2016).

This example reflects thinking about animals in a way that goes beyond how the animals serve and/or benefit humans. Patty Born (2024) highlights the value of such thinking in her book *Multispecies Thinking in the Classroom and Beyond*. Born discusses how everyday entanglements with the other-than-human elements of the Earth (plants, animals, places, and systems) can challenge and expand our worldview. Such entanglements, while often physical, are also emotional and philosophical. Multispecies thinking calls for a "re-think" regarding the role of humans and our relationship with the other-than-human world. It also calls for a "re-think" of how we identify ourselves as individuals.

Authentic Dialogue

One way to help children expand and test their philosophical ideas is to engage them in authentic dialogue about those ideas. Authentic dialogue is a form of communication that is genuine and open. People engaged in authentic dialogue aren't trying to impress or convince others. They listen attentively and seek to understand another person's perspective. People engaged in authentic dialogue seek connection and growth.

Authentic dialogue is a form of "real talk" that is open-ended and directed by the speakers. Engaging young children in real talk includes letting them know that their thoughts and ideas will be respected and giving them time to engage in both adult–child and child–child dialogue. While adult–child interaction can be rich and instructive, child–child dialogue has a special uniqueness and originality. A child telling another child that "every tree has a different song", for example, may be more impactful and engaging than the child's giving this same message to an adult. The child–child dialogue may go something like this:

Child 1: Did you know that every tree has a different song? Listen. (Child 1 uses a stick to tap on two different trees.)
Child 2: I think I heard it. Let me try. (Child 2 taps on two different trees.) You have to be really quiet to hear it.
Child 1: I wonder why the trees sound different.
Child 2: Maybe one tree has thicker bark.
Child 1: Or maybe there's something different inside the tree.
Child 2: We have to be careful when we tap on the tree. We don't want to hurt it.
Child 1: Right. If we hurt it, it might not make a song again.

This exchange between two children reflects observation, curiosity, conjecture, and respect. It also reflects philosophical and scientific thinking as well as ecological perspective taking.

Philosophical inquiry and ecological perspective taking may also promote prospective thinking, another important aspect of education for sustainability at the early childhood level. Prospective thinking involves thinking in terms of "what if." This form of thinking "implies a transformation from thinking about the actual into thinking about the possible" (Pramling & Pramling Samuelsson 2025, pp. 211–212).

Prospective thinking is a critical component of sustainability in that it allows us to imagine how things could be different. It may also provide some direction in terms of what to do in the creation of a more desirable future. In the early childhood classroom, what-if thinking might be initiated by the teacher, but it can also be initiated by the children. Authentic dialogue is perhaps the most effective context for supporting prospective thinking.

Cree and Robb (2021) offer some guidelines for authentic dialogue. They highlight the importance of "informal enquiry dialogue" as a path to building relationships that are more trusting. They note how the way we communicate with children can either help or stymie the relationship and the meaning-making process. Cree and Robb encourage educators to enter into children's dialogue versus setting an agenda for dialogue. They note how "adult agenda-led" dialogue can actually be threatening to young learners. The children may feel "put on the spot" to come up with the right answers or to suggest only "appropriate" ideas.

Authentic dialogue, on the other hand, co-evolves around the creative exploration of ideas. Marietta McCarty (2006) offers some suggestions on how to make this happen when working with a group of children. She emphasizes the importance of "talking together," of including everyone in the conversation. She notes how "talking together" differs from a game of tag, which is all about tagging others out. In "talking together," the intent is keeping everyone in.

One way to keep everyone in the discussion is to establish some simple "rules" or guidelines for group discussion. McCarty (2006) refers to these as "requests" and offers just two: "Never speak when someone else is talking" and "Never make fun of what someone says." These requests are about active listening and respect for the ideas of others. She limits her requests to just these two "because they are simple and easy to remember" (pp. xvii–xviii).

Using a dialogic reading approach when sharing children's books is an excellent way to stimulate authentic dialogue and philosophical thinking. Dialogic reading basically means children and adults having a conversation about a book. With dialogic reading, children become actively involved in the telling and interpreting of the story. Dialogic reading helps children develop language and literacy skills. It also "promotes children's perspective-taking skills by enabling them to focus on the emotional and mental states of the characters in the story" (Yurdakul, Beyazit & Ayhan 2025, p. 49).

Ecological Identity

We often use the term "self-concept" in reference to how we view ourselves. In describing this view – whether to ourselves or others – we might focus on one or more aspects of our self-concept, such as our emotional/psychological self ("I am a happy person") or our physical self ("I am athletic"). Whether we think about it or not, we also have an ecological self (sometimes referred to as "ecological identity"). Philosophical thinking can contribute to the development of a healthy ecological self, especially when paired with mindfulness in nature. As discussed in the previous chapter, mindfulness in nature can help children develop a deeper awareness of the world and their relationship with it (Schein 2018). Through mindfulness and philosophical thinking, children can become aware of the oneness of the natural world and know that they are part of something so much bigger than themselves.

As indicated in previous chapters, the focus of the ecological self is on connections with and attitudes towards the natural environment. We may see ourselves as separate from and/or superior to the rest of the natural world. A person with a healthy ecological identity, however, views self as part of the natural world (Wang 2017). This view of self is consistent with the "land ethic" articulated by Aldo Leopold: "A land ethic changes the role of Homo Sapiens from conqueror of the land-community to plain member and citizen of it" (Leopold, 1949/1986, p. 240). The "land-community" as defined by Leopold includes soils, waters, plants, and animals.

Viewing one's self as part of (versus separate from) the rest of the natural world is also consistent with the long-held beliefs of many Indigenous People. Words from a speech by Chief Seattle are often quoted as an expression of this belief: "The earth does not belong to man, man belongs to the earth…. Man did not weave the web of life, he is merely a strand in it."

Existential Intelligence

Some children seem to be more philosophical in their thinking and interests than others. We see differences in other areas of development, including types of intelligence. The theory of "multiple intelligences" developed by Howard Gardner calls attention to the fact that intelligence consists of more than what is typically measured on standard IQ tests. Originally, Gardner (1983) introduced the idea of seven types of intelligence (linguistic, mathematical/logical, spatial, kinaesthetic, musical, interpersonal, and intrapersonal). He has since added an eighth intelligence – the naturalistic intelligence – and suggested that there may be a ninth, which he refers to as "existential intelligence" (Checkley 1997).

The existential intelligence reflects a proclivity to ask philosophical questions, or questions relating to the meaning of existence. Existential intelligence is engaged as we ponder the underlying truths of our existence. What do our lives mean? Where do we fit in with the rest of the universe? Pondering these questions can influence our individual and collective ecological identities. Encouraging philosophical thinking about the natural world can promote not only young children's existential and naturalistic intelligences but their spiritual development as well.

Questions about the Mysteries of Life

Young children are good at asking questions. Some of their questions are scientific in nature. Are the clouds filled with water? Why do some trees grow faster than others? Some questions are more philosophical and address what may be considered the "mysteries of life." Why do some people do bad things? What happens after we die? Do trees feel sad when they get old? We may struggle to answer these questions in a way that feels honest and authentic. We may be concerned about how to respect the child's inquiring mind and wonder what is appropriate to the child's intellectual, emotional, and spiritual development. We may also be concerned about respecting the beliefs and values of the child's family. The following discussion may be helpful in addressing these concerns.

What children need and want from us when they ask questions about the mysteries of life aren't definitive or clear-cut answers. What they really want is an appreciation of wonder and wondering. They want someone to be with them as they ponder the mysteries of the world around them – mysteries that can be felt but not explained. Mystery, in this context, refers to the experience of realities that seem to be incomprehensible. Being aware of realities beyond their current understanding is an expected part of childhood. Some of what they don't understand at the present time will become clear as they get older (e.g., why can't we see the sun at night). Other questions they wonder about will always remain a mystery. It's good to know that an appreciation of mystery is one of the characteristics of spirituality.

The recognition of mystery needs to be nurtured and matured rather than dismissed as infantile thinking. "Mystery-sensing" is part of spirituality (Hyde 2008), with a role to play at every stage of an individual's life. Mystery and soulfulness tend to overlap. They can also reinforce each other. Mystery can deepen one's soulfulness, while soulfulness, in turn, can embolden us to embrace mystery.

"Mystery-sensing" often occurs during experiences of awe and wonder. It's not only important for children to have such experiences; they also need time and support to reflect on these experiences. Reflection is one of the core components of philosophical thinking. (See Box 10.2. for guidelines on how to encourage philosophical thinking with young children.)

Conclusion

Children need frequent rich and varied experiences in natural environments to develop a positive relationship with nature. They also need time and support to ponder the meaning of such experiences. The process of meaning-making deepens young children's sense of connectedness to nature and contributes to their spiritual development. Philosophical thinking is one avenue available to children for developing an appreciation of the wonders and mysteries of the world in which we live.

BOX 10.2   SUGGESTIONS: GUIDELINES FOR FOSTERING PHILOSOPHICAL THINKING

While philosophical thinking comes naturally to young children, there are ways that we, as adults, can support this important aspect of meaning-making. Here are ten guidelines for doing so.

1. Encourage curiosity.
2. Use a dialogic (based on dialogue) approach when sharing books and stories with children.
3. Follow the children's interests in planning activities.
4. Model philosophical thinking.
5. Invite and model "I wonder …" statements.
6. Support the children in making "I Wonder" books.
7. Invite the children to draw, sing, dance, and paint their ideas and feelings about the world of nature.
8. Really listen to children and take their ideas seriously.
9. Give children time and opportunity to engage in dialogue with each other.
10. Engage children in meaningful conversations about such philosophical topics as peace, kindness, happiness, and friendship.

11

Wonder, Aesthetics, and the Creative Arts

Creativity, the Creative Arts, and Spirituality

Nature for a young child is often a source of wonder. A snowfall, a strawberry ripening on the vine, a leaf floating in a bucket of water – such ordinary phenomena can bring joy to a child. Witnessing and responding to such wonders can nurture the spiritual development of young children. The creative arts can be used as an avenue for responding to the wonders of the world in which we live.

Creative arts are a form of human expression involving creativity and imagination. While the creative arts may involve language (as in poetry and drama), some forms – such as drawing, painting, music, and dance – are not bound by language and may be especially suited to the interests and abilities of young children. Different forms of the creative arts provide opportunities for children to express and deepen their insights about the world around them. The creative arts can also help children connect with their emotions and feelings.

Creativity plays a pivotal role in human growth and development. "The urge to create is a fundamental human drive through which we can explore our identities, push our capabilities, find purpose and meaning, and lead more enriching lives" (Manjeera, Gundu & Rao 2024, p. 369). The creative potential of individuals is also an important dimension of spirituality (Goodliff 2013).

"Creativity, like spirituality, has multiple meanings" (Goodliff 2013, p. 1057) and shows up in multiple ways in the lives of young children. Creativity is often evident in the way young children play, especially play involving the imagination and fantasy. It shows up, too, in children's curiosity and their propensity for exploring possibilities. Creativity is evident in the way that young children enthusiastically participate in arts-based activities. Watch children as they paint, sing, and dance, and you'll see a type of engagement that connects thought, emotion, and action. You'll see children engaged in a meaning-making activity.

Creativity has been described as "intelligence having fun." Engaging in the creative arts can, indeed, be enjoyable, but the benefits of doing so often extend beyond simply having fun. Engaging in creative activities can awaken the soul, which, in this context, can include transcending the ordinary sense of self.

Self-transcendence tends to occur when a person is in a "state of flow," which is sometimes experienced while engaged in a creative activity. This "state" or experience might be described as being so completely absorbed or engrossed in what you are doing or what you are experiencing that the sense of a separate self is replaced with an experience of oneness. Flow theory suggests that flow is a state that people enter when they engage in an activity that is intrinsically motivated. For young children, flow may be experienced as entering a "new" or "magic world" (Moula, Palmer & Walshe 2022).

Post-humanist thought suggests that intra-connectedness may contribute to the flow experience. A flow experience in nature, for example, is viewed as being co-created, with nature playing an active role in the process. The "flow state is not something that a human experiences and achieves, but is something that emerges in between the material-multispecies assemblages we might become entangled with/in" (Hankin & Hogarth 2025, p. 18).

BOX 11.1 REFLECTIONS: AESTHETICS AND A SENSE OF WONDER

(Originally published in *Exchange* 2010, May/June; used with permission.)

Rachel Carson (1956) – scientist, writer, and environmentalist – tells us that "A child's world is fresh and new and beautiful, full of wonder and excitement" (p. 42). Many of us have heard and been inspired by these words but may not have a clear idea about what wonder really is. This isn't surprising, because wonder in different contexts can mean different things. As used by Carson (1956), wonder refers to a "clear-eyed vision," a "true instinct for what is beautiful and awe-inspiring" (p. 42). Wonder in this context is something we feel (an emotion) but also a 'way of knowing' based on intuition or natural instinct.

Wonder as an Emotion

Emotions are what give zest to life, and quality and meaning to our existence. Some might say that emotions are what make life worth living. Yet some emotions (such as anger, jealousy, disgust, and sadness) may leave us feeling miserable. Wonder is different; it's an emotion that uplifts and inspires. We can count on wonder to enrich and ennoble our lives. As Carson (1956) says, wonder can serve "as an unfailing antidote against the boredom and disenchantments of later years, the sterile preoccupation with things that are artificial, the alienation from the sources of our strength" (p. 43).

We experience wonder as a spark inside of us – a spark that lights up our life and stirs our imagination. We also experience wonder as an emotion that takes us outside of ourselves and into a realm that is greater than ourselves. When strongly felt, this experience of "being outside of ourselves" – and outside of time – is sometimes referred to as ecstasy and is accompanied by intense joy or delight (Hart 2006).

Beauty seems to play a special role in awakening our sense of wonder and allowing us to experience 'self-forgetting' moments of great joy and ecstasy (Johnson 2002). Beauty can also lead us to an understanding of truth. The poet John Keats writes, "Beauty is truth, truth beauty – that is all ye know on earth, and all ye need to know."

Wonder as a Way of Knowing

We usually relate the concept of truth to something that conforms to fact or actuality, something that can be proven or arrived at through rational thought. We can thank poets, like Keats, for giving us other ideas about the meaning of truth. By equating beauty and truth and linking this to a type of knowing, Keats' words can help us appreciate another aspect of wonder – that is, wonder as a way of knowing. The type of knowing associated with wonder isn't primarily about thinking; it's more intuitive than rational and involves a "direct knowing" (Hart 2006).

Children and Wonder

The sense of wonder seems to be much more pronounced in children than in adults (Carson 1956; Hart 2006). We see this in the way young children respond to and interact with certain elements of nature. Watch young children as it begins to snow or as they play in a pile of leaves. You'll witness an abundance of exuberance and joy. You'll see children wholly engaged in the now, and you'll find them responding with their whole bodies. They'll laugh, dance, run, listen, and perhaps even taste.

Adults, on the other hand, are more likely to respond with thoughts about what comes next. They tend to spend little time immersing themselves in the moment and in the sensory experiences of what is happening around them. Adults see the snow and think of shovelling the driveway or become anxious about driving on icy roads. They see the leaves and think of all the raking that needs to be done.

Children's way of relating to the world corresponds to their unique way of knowing the world – a way based more on wonder than analytical thought. Children know the world – especially the natural environment – in a deep and direct manner, not as a background for events. For children, the natural world is never formal or abstract, nor is it a scene or a landscape (Cobb 1977; Sebba 1991). Unfortunately, this way of knowing the world tends to dissipate over time. During the early stages of cognitive development – when learning is dependent on concrete perceptual experiences – perception conducts thought. With adults, however, perception obeys thought (Sebba 1991). With this shift, the sense of wonder usually diminishes rather quickly.

Adults would do well to recognize and honour children's way of knowing and strive to keep the children's and their own sense of wonder alive. Wonder, as Carson (1956) says, can serve as a lifelong source of joy and enrichment. Wonder can also stimulate the imagination and serve as motivation for further learning (Cobb 1977; Wilson 2008). It may even be possible that it is only through wonder that we come to know the world as it really is (Wilson 2008).

Children, Wonder, and Aesthetic Experiences

In working with young children, we often acknowledge the importance of aesthetic development. We provide opportunities for them to experience beauty, we draw attention to beautiful things, and we encourage children to create and represent beauty through the mediums of art, dance, and music. These efforts are based on the understanding that putting children in touch with beauty will enrich their lives and foster their sense of wonder. Aesthetic experiences do, indeed, provide these benefits for children. But there are other benefits as well – some quite powerful in their potential impact on both children and society.

Providing aesthetic experiences and fostering their sense of wonder can help children see 'potential beauty' as well as the beauty being experienced in the moment. While children gain inspiration and enjoyment from being in touch with beauty, their 'sense of possibility' can also be nurtured and strengthened. This sense of possibility enables children to see a future different from what exists at present, including the possibility of seeing beauty in places now filled with ugliness and seeing peace and harmony in places now filled with anger and discord. Along with this sense of possibility is the motivation to encourage further beauty into existence. The words of the Sufi poet Rumi remind us of this possibility: "Let the beauty we love be what we do" (Rumi 1997).

Aesthetics includes the capacity to sense, appreciate, and respond emotionally to beauty in both human creations and the natural environment (Kemple & Johnson 2002). When we reflect on the sources of beauty, we often limit our thinking to the physical manifestations of it – whether this is in human creations or the natural environment. There are, of course, social aspects to each as well, and these social aspects can manifest great beauty and awaken a sense of wonder. Examples of human generosity and kindness come to mind, as do the social behaviours of elephants and dolphins. Certainly, the complex workings of bees and the dedication evident as birds feed and protect their young are other examples of beauty in the social aspects of the natural environment. Whether in human creations or the natural environment, whether in physical manifestations or social realms, early aesthetic experiences are powerful and can have lasting significance (Kemple & Johnson 2002).

Living with Wonder

For many of us, that marvellous gift of wonder we enjoyed when we were children diminishes or vanishes over time (Carson 1956). Perhaps this concern is what prompted

Abraham Heschel to write, "I did not ask for success; I asked for wonder" (Heschel 1983).

To keep the spark of wonder burning in our daily lives, it may be helpful to consider how children experience wonder. They remain present in the now, they open all their senses to what they're experiencing, and they engage their hearts – not just their minds – as they experience and reflect on the world around them. With some effort, we can do this, too. For example, when taking a walk, or just spending time outdoors, we can make a conscious effort to really 'take in' everything around us. We can make a point of noticing sounds, scents, colours, temperatures, patterns of light and shadow, the shape of clouds, the presence and behaviour of insects, subtle changes from one place to another or from one time to another. Such concentrated attention can help us see and experience things in new ways. It can help us find beauty in ordinary, overlooked places and experience inspiration and wonder in what otherwise we might consider commonplace.

Another way to keep the spark of wonder alive is to surround ourselves with beauty. In *The Little Prince*, we read that since something is beautiful, it is truly useful (de Saint-Exupéry 1943). That which is beautiful may not always be useful in the sense of what is most efficient or most readily available. But things and places of beauty can be useful to us in ways which efficiency and expediency can never offer. The architect Frank Lloyd Wright once noted that if we foolishly ignore beauty, we will soon find ourselves without it – and without beauty, our lives are impoverished. Investing in beauty, he noted, would give us something of value that would remain with us all the days of our lives.

We know that some things of beauty – like kittens, fresh flowers, and warm oatmeal cookies – may not always retain their freshness. Having once experienced their beauty, however, can enrich our lives over a long period of time. As Louise Chawla (1990) once noted, the spaces and views that we experience as children become inner landscapes or "ecstatic memories" which remain with us "like radioactive jewels buried within us, emitting energy across the years of our life" (Chawla 1990, p. 18). It would seem that 'ecstatic memories' and the energy they impart need not be confined to what we experience as children. Perhaps deep encounters with beauty – experienced at any age – can reap similar benefits.

References

Carson, R. (1956). *The Sense of Wonder*. Harper & Row.

Chawla, L. (1990). Ecstatic places. *Children's Environments Quarterly*, 7(4), 18–23.

Cobb, E. (1977). *The Ecology of Imagination in Childhood*. Columbia University Press.

de Saint-Exupéry, A. (1943). *The Little Prince*. Harcourt Books.

Hart, T. (2006). Spiritual experiences and capacities of children and youth. In E. C. Rhehlkepartain, P. E. King, L. Wagener, and P. L. Benson (Eds.). *The Handbook of Spiritual Development in Childhood and Adolescence* (pp. 163–178). Sage Publications.

Heschel, A. (1983). *I Asked for Wonder*. Crossroad Publishing.

Johnson, B. (2002). On the spiritual benefits of wilderness. *International Journal of Wilderness*, 8(3), 28–32.

Keats, J. *Ode on a Grecian Urn*. http://www.bartleby.com/101/625.html (retrieved February 4, 2025).

Kemple, K. M., & Johnson, C. A. (2002). From the inside out: Nurturing aesthetic response to nature in the primary grades. *Childhood Education*, 78(4).

Rumi, J. (1997). *The Essential Rumi*. HarperOne.

Sebba, R. (1991). The landscapes of childhood – The reflection of childhood's environment in adult memories and in children's attitudes. *Environment and Behavior*, 23(4), 395–422.

Wilson, R. (2008). *Nature and Young Children*. Routledge.

Wilson, R.A. (retrieved January 21, 2010).

http://www.earlychildhoodnews.com/earlychildhood/article_view.aspx?ArticleId=70

Nature and the Creative Arts

There are many reasons to integrate nature and the creative arts. Nature not only offers rich opportunities for children to engage in the creative arts but also invites and is responsive to children's creativity. Additionally, children are innately drawn to the natural world, and the aesthetic elements of nature are readily available.

Engaging with the arts is basically a meaning-making process. Artistic activities help children make meaning about the world and their place in the world. While research on the interconnection of nature and the arts for young children is still somewhat limited, studies that have been conducted support nature-inspired art activities as an avenue for enhancing the well-being of children while promoting environmental sustainability (Kalafati, Flogaiti & Daskolia 2025; O'Gorman 2024; Ruokonen & Lepisto 2024).

Increasing reports about the number of children feeling unhappy or experiencing isolation and loneliness since the COVID-19 pandemic led a team of researchers to conduct a review of the literature for evidence of nature-based art activities promoting the mental health and well-being of children (Moula, Palmer & Walshe 2022). The researchers identified eight published studies on this topic. The included studies involved a total of 602 children and young people from five different countries. The nature-based art activities described in these studies included drawing, music, and sculpting.

The most frequently reported positive outcomes for the children related to connectedness to nature and a sense of well-being. The well-being outcomes included increased empathy, emotional regulation, positive mood, and self-perception. Positive outcomes included decreased stress levels and improvements in autonomy, agency, sense of authenticity, and sense of belonging in nature. The nature-based art activities led the children to "gradually perceive themselves as part of the environment, and the environment as part of themselves" (Moula, Palmer & Walshe 2022, p. 13).

Suggestions for Integrating Nature and the Creative Arts

The following discussion includes some ideas about how to combine nature and the creative arts through the mediums of drawing/painting/sculpting, music, and movement. Poetry and other forms of literature as additional areas of the creative arts are discussed in Chapter 12.

Drawing, Painting, and Sculpting

The author Amy Tan is probably best known for her novel *The Joy Luck Club*, which was published in 1989. Readers may be surprised to learn that her book *The Backyard Bird Chronicles* (Tan 2024) is non-fiction and includes her detailed drawings of birds. One of the comments that Tan made during an interview about this book focused on the value of drawing. Drawing, she said, is the best way to closely observe. Tan notes how beauty is constantly all around us but often hidden in plain sight. Drawing, she says, helps us pay attention to – or discover – that beauty. Michael Parr, president of the American Bird Conservancy, says basically the same thing. In a review of Tan's book, Parr (2024) writes, "If you really want to understand something, draw it."

Not only do drawing, painting, and sculpting help us discover the intricacies of what is right in front of us, but engaging in these art activities can instil a greater appreciation of the spiritual dimensions of everyday life. The process of drawing, painting, and sculpting with natural materials involves observation, inquiry, and attention to what makes something unique. This process can easily strengthen children's attention to the beauty and wonders of the natural world. Representing what is perceived isn't about creating a replica of something in nature. It's about entering more deeply into a relationship with the object of observation.

Guidelines for best practices in early childhood education have often highlighted the process as being more important than the product in art experiences for young children. To this, we should add the need to focus more on the relationship with the materials that are used than on what is produced. This focus is consistent with a post-humanistic approach to education which emphasizes respectful relationships with natural materials rather than treating them as commodities.

"The use and abuse of natural materials" is something that Sue Elliott has addressed numerous times in her long career in early childhood education. In a discussion about the use of plant materials in art activities, Sue asked, "Can we use natural materials without paint or glue for ephemeral artwork, art that can be dismantled and returned to the environment intact and unscathed?" (Elliott 2025). Sue raised similar questions in a book she published in 1997, *Snails Live in Houses Too*. As the title of this book suggests, the way we relate to the natural world should include an awareness and concern for the more-than-human world.

Sue notes how children's engagement with natural materials can be informative and enjoyable without causing harm. She describes how manipulating round river stones, for example, could lead to knowledge about their formation and sensory properties and promote observational and classification skills. Sue values the knowledge and skills obtained through the manipulation of natural materials but highlights the importance of also attending to attitudes about the environment. "Attitudes could be developed whereby stones are seen as beautiful objects with an important role to play in the environment through erosion" (Elliott & Emmett 1997, p. 41).

Sue questions such nature-based art activities as painting rocks and pasting leaves. She urges early childhood educators to consider "why they are using natural materials and what uses are acceptable in terms of the environment" (Elliott & Emmett 1997, p. 42). In addressing teachers, she asks,

> Have you ever talked to children about the need to care for the natural materials they use? About how you borrowed them from the environment for a short time and will return them to the environment? About how we need to appreciate them for their inherent properties?
> (Elliott & Emmett 1997, p. 41)

What Sue is basically saying is that we need to consider the ethical aspects of how we use natural materials and be mindful of the messages we give to children in the process.

Music and Music Making

Music as a universal language doesn't rely on a specific vocabulary or grammar to convey meaning. Music uses rhythm, melody, and harmony to express and evoke universal understandings and emotions. Music, as a form of the creative arts, can be accessed and appreciated by people of all backgrounds. The meaning and messages expressed through music transcend cultural, linguistic, and social boundaries. Music speaks to the soul more than to the mind.

Music can be used to help young children tune in to the wonders of nature. An appreciation of these wonders can inspire children to make music of their own. Just listening to the music of nature can nurture sensitivity to nature and deeper connections with nature. While most children are familiar with the idea of birds singing, they may not have considered the idea of listening for music in the buzzing of insects, the rustling of leaves, branches rubbing against each other, rain tapping on the window, or water flowing over rocks. By listening intently to the music made by birds, insects, wind, and rain, children become better observers of the natural world.

Children's nature connectedness can also be strengthened by encouraging them to use natural materials to make their own musical instruments. A container with a lid and some seeds or small pebbles can be used to make a shaker. Shakers are not only easy to make, they're also easy to use as an accompaniment to singing and dancing. Sticks, grass, and water can also be used to make simple musical instruments.

Deborah Schein (2018) used a small plastic container and a few pinecones and acorns to make a "nature rattle" which she calls a "nattle." Young children delight in playing with this simple toy, including using it as a shaker in making music.

Clemens Arvay (2018a) suggests making musical instruments from dried gourds. He notes how, while gourds can be used to make simple rattles, they can also be crafted into more sophisticated musical instruments, such as kalimbas (finger piano) or didgeridoo (ancient traditional instrument of the Australian Aboriginal people).

Just as making music *from* nature can be a rewarding experience for children, so can playing music *in* nature. Such outdoor musical instruments as marimbas and slap drums can be used outdoors by children of all abilities. One study investigating the impact of music making outdoors found that primary-age children experienced feelings of joy, connection, wonder, awe, and a sense of inner calm or peace both during and after the music-making activity. Some of the children described the experience as entering a "new world" and feeling a sense of interconnectivity or harmony with nature. The children indicated that making music together outdoors also helped them feel more bonded with each other and their surroundings (Adams & Beauchamp 2019). One early childhood educator, in discussing the benefits of music, described how music allows children to experience "the joy of just 'being' at the moment" (Rouse & Hyde 2024, p. 9). The results of these studies highlight the understanding that making music outdoors surrounded by nature can take children to a place where they experience spiritual moments.

Creative Movement/Dance

Young children need little encouragement to move about in natural outdoor environments. They roll down hills, stomp in puddles, climb over logs, and dig in the sand. Adding nature-inspired dance and dance improvisation to their movement repertoire can open up new ways of knowing, understanding, and being in the natural world. Creative movement can also give young children an avenue for expressing how they feel about the world of nature.

Nature-inspired movement can be as simple as imitating what is observed in nature – a leaf twisting on a branch or falling from a tree, a butterfly or bird moving from flower to flower, a bush swaying in the wind, a rabbit hopping through the grass, and so on. These imitative movements can encourage closer observation and appreciation of the ways things work in nature. They can also inspire wonder and wondering.

Nature-inspired movement and dance can also be used to enhance children's understandings about specific aspects of the human/nature connection. In one case, a concern about children's limited understanding and sometimes troublesome relationship with weather indicated a need for a new approach to learning about the weather. Too often, weather is something to be studied rather than experienced. Improvisational dance was introduced as an innovative way to interrupt or offer an alternative to human-centred and/or abstract learning about weather. The intent of this improvisational dance activity with young children was to counteract the positioning of weather "as simply a background context to everyday activities" (Pollitt, Blaise & Rooney 2021, p. 1145). The focus was on learning *with* the weather, not just *about* the weather.

This improvisational dance started with a guided activity in which children were asked to lie on the floor with their hands on their tummies. They were then asked to think about what kinds of weather they felt inside their bodies. The children readily responded with such descriptors as "Stormy," "Sunny," and "Snowing." After the children were attuned to thinking about weather as something in their own body, they were asked to focus on their breath, to notice the movement of air in and out of their own bodies. Children were also invited to use their arms and hands to scoop the air around them – to scoop it into their mouths, to fold it over their heads and their shoulders. The children were soon "swallowing and wallowing in small weather worlds plucked from the air around them" (Pollitt, Blaise & Rooney 2021, p. 1146).

The dance was paused and a question asked, "Where do you think weathers live?" The children's first responses suggested that weather exists outside the classroom. After a moment of reflection, however, the children decided that it's inside as well – even inside themselves. Later, when asked, "What does weather breathe?" it wasn't surprising that some of the children responded "Us!" What the children experienced at that moment was "multiple weather bodies breathing together" (Pollitt, Blaise & Rooney 2021, p. 1146). This improvised movement activity allowed the children to develop a more nuanced, integrated, and kinaesthetic understanding of weather systems than what could be achieved through "a disconnected, disembodied learning 'about' the weather via indoor diagram charts" (p. 1149).

BOX 11.2   PROGRAM SPOTLIGHT: RUNNING WILD

Several community organizations in Australia worked together in the planning, implementation, and evaluation of a nature-based arts program they called "Running Wild." The organizations involved included a community theatre group, a primary school, and the Royal Botanic Gardens. Individuals working with the project included local artists, scientists, and Indigenous Elders. The aim of the project was to introduce students to a nature reserve ("The Pines") near their school through art-making activities.

Thirty-six students participated in the Running Wild program 12 times over a five-week period. During this time, they were introduced to both Western and Indigenous perspectives of ecology within the reserve. Activities in the reserve included tree planting, constructing a village of "bush cubbies," and making spirit animal costumes. The students also made a short film and created an outdoor exhibition about the reserve.

Most of the participating students live in neighbourhoods with high levels of socio-economic disadvantage and spend most of their time outside of school playing video games or watching television. At the beginning of the project, many students showed a strong resistance to being outside in nature and had remarkably low fitness levels.

Over time, the students became more comfortable in the natural environment and began to express their capacity for agency and independence in the environment. They also became more comfortable and skilled in working together on collaborative activities. Assessment results at the end of the project showed increased nature connection on the part of the children and a significant positive effect on their mental well-being. Results also showed enhanced learning abilities and a deeper understanding of biodiversity and the importance of native plants and animals.

Reference

Beer, T., Cook, A. & Kantor, K. (2018b). Running Wild: Engaging and empowering future custodians of place through creative nature-based play. *Journal of Public Pedagogies*, 3, 5–19.

Conclusion

There are numerous benefits of nature-based creative arts activities for young children, including enhancing the spiritual dimensions of children's connectedness to nature. Every child should have multiple opportunities to participate in a variety of nature-based creative arts activities at home and at school. While the activities may be as simple as dancing with the wind, the results can nourish a young child's soul.

12

Stories, Poems, and Storytelling

Stories and the Messages They Carry

Stories – whether they are about the past, present, or future – carry messages about who we are and who we might become. Stories also carry messages about the world around us and our relationship with it.

"Telling the Holy," an essay by Scott Russell Sanders (2016), speaks to the importance of story in connecting us to place. As Sanders explains, stories can reveal ways in which a "spiritual landscape does indeed flicker and flame within the physical one" (p. 9). The title of his essay – "Telling the Holy" – is based on the Apache word for myth which translates as "to tell the holiness" (p. 9).

"Telling the holy" isn't just about "sacred stories" told in a religious context. "Telling the holy" includes myths and legends rooted in different cultural traditions. Some such narratives are intentionally used to convey moral teachings and the beliefs of a community. Such stories can lead to a greater appreciation of diverse cultures and help shape cultural identity. Some stories give messages about the spiritual dimensions of connectedness to nature. These stories can play an important role in keeping our hearts and spirits strong.

Stories are a more powerful force in shaping attitudes and values than the giving of information. This is especially true for children. Eco-themed stories – or pro-nature literature – can be used with young children to foster ecological literacy and to promote positive attitudes about the environment. Ecological literacy means the ability to understand and care for the natural world and its systems.

Interviews with professionals in the fields of ecotourism, conservation, and education indicate that "storytelling works as an interpretative tool which stimulates preschool children's imagination and supports not only learning about, but also with nature" (King, García-Rosell & Noakes 2020, p. 7). The term "ecological storytelling" is used in this context to highlight the effectiveness of storytelling in helping children realize that they are part of nature, not separate from it. As expressed by one interviewee, "We've given it [ecological storytelling] a name because it's so important to us" (p. 7).

Eco-Literacy and Children's Literature

Eco-literacy (or ecological literacy) is more than a cognitive ability and involves more than reading the written word. Eco-literacy integrates emotional, social, and ecological intelligence and thus can be used to promote sustainable living.

Children's stories about the natural world and the human relationship with it have changed over time. Children's literature during the nature study movement of the late 19th century included stories promoting understanding and appreciation of nature and the way it works. Many of these stories were also designed to cultivate the child's imagination and promote care of the environment.

A shift in the focus of children's literature occurred at the turn of the 20th century. Messages about competition rather than environmental stewardship became more evident, as did "a disregard for the well-being of nonhuman species" (op de Beeck 2018, p. 74). Children's authors and gatekeepers, at the time, were at pains to present an upbeat account of industrial expansion and species habitat loss. These efforts and the messages they carried reflect "the fairy tale of modernity" (op de Beeck 2018, p. 74), which supports the idea that the land can be sacrificed for desired industrial innovations.

A study conducted a few years ago focused on the images and messages presented in non-fiction children's books that relate in some way to sustainability. Unfortunately, the results weren't encouraging. At least 50% of the images depicted humans as consumers. Even images of humans involved in conservation activities often depicted such post-consumer activities as recycling (Muthukrishnan & Kelly 2017). Such images raise concerns about an overemphasis on consumerism as a way of life. While young children should be taught the value of recycling and reusing, they should also be introduced to other positive ways of interacting with the rest of the natural world in non-consumerist ways, such as using rain barrels and growing or foraging for food.

Another study analysed nearly 300 picture books receiving the Caldecott Medal from 1938 to 2008. Findings showed decreasing images of natural environments or natural elements and increasing images of built environments. Over time, the images of the built environments became more dominant – that is, they changed from being a mere presence to being the primary focus of the illustration. There were only a few images of humans interacting with the rest of nature in a positive way (Williams et al. 2012).

Pro-Nature Books

Issues to consider when choosing books to share with children include the ways in which children, nature, and the human–nature relationship are depicted. Ideally, children are portrayed as agents of change and nature presented as an integral part of daily life versus something to be visited, studied, and used. Messages about the human–nature relationship should focus on kinship and compassion versus dominance and control. Multispecies awareness is another feature to look for in choosing nature-themed books for children. Such awareness "recognizes humans as connected and part-of, rather than simply the centre of, a network here to serve our needs" (Born 2024, p. 3). Multispecies awareness decentres the human in the human–nature relationship.

Ideas on how to promote multispecies awareness through children's literature can be found in *Multispecies Thinking in the Classroom and Beyond* (Born 2024). A chapter on eco-literacy by Maggie Struck and Patty Born includes guidelines on how to choose children's books that support multispecies awareness. Their guidelines include looking for books that support children in deepening their relations with other species and that promote their sense of agency and self-efficacy.

> Books should present children as having power to positively and directly impact their surroundings. Those that portray children helping plants and animals in developmentally appropriate, realistic ways can be beneficial in children's thinking about their own agency as well as their relationships with and their responsibility toward other species.
> (Struck & Born 2024, p. 61)

Books with positive messages about nature and positive relationships between humans and the rest of the natural world might be referred to as "pro-nature books" (Wilson 2016, 2018). Pro-nature books usually include one or more of the following attributes:

- ♦ Portrays nature as something more than a resource for humans
- ♦ Provides an accurate account of nature and the way it works
- ♦ Offers some ideas about how humans can relate to the rest of nature in respectful, caring, reciprocal ways.

Working with others to care for the environment is something else to look for in choosing nature-themed books with young children. Two such books are highlighted by Struck and Born

(2024): *City Green* (DiSalvo-Ryan 2019) and *We Are the Water Protectors* (Lindstorm & Goade 2021). Books portraying children working with others in sustainability efforts can stimulate hope about moving towards a more sustainable future. When children see that they are not alone in caring for the environment, they are more likely to feel hopeful and motivated.

Another feature to look for in nature-themed books for children relates to the role of humans in the story. Some children's books present nature as something separate from human society. Such books may present nature as no more than a resource for humans – to be used for material gain and/or recreation or to be analysed and studied. Some books may present nature as a force working against humans or as a force that humans need to control or constrain. These human-centred messages are in opposition to the eco-centric messages of pro-nature books. Eco-centric messages reflect a post-humanistic philosophy highlighting interdependence and reciprocity versus separateness in the relationship between humans and the rest of the natural world.

Where the Wild Things Are (Sendeck 1963) is a good example of how post-humanism can be expressed in children's literature. Post-humanism "is embodied by 'the rumpus,' a primal celebration of wildness and a reflection of the human need to retain and perform animality in order to be connected to the natural world" (Harju & Rouse 2018, p. 456).

The Blueberry List is an excellent resource for identifying pro-nature books for children. The Blueberry Award, organized and administered by the Evanston Public Library in Illinois (USA), honours children's books that inspire a love of nature and action for planet Earth.

Animal Stories

Animal stories tend to be especially popular with young children. Alison Hawthorne Deming (2014), in her collection of essays on animals and the human spirit, writes about how, when she was young, animal stories could make her feel "wonderstruck." She writes, "I could feel my responses to animals inviting me into continuity and connection with forces larger than myself." This "transcendent function", she says, can take us "back home in the old web of connections from which we have sprung and feel once again that we belong" (p. 64).

One feature to look for in choosing animal stories to share with young children relates to the depiction of animals living in their own world versus being managed, manipulated, or used by humans. Unfortunately, some animal stories reinforce "our habit of thinking anthropocentrically and our failure to imagine animals' own experiences" (op de Beeck 2018, p. 81).

Anthropomorphism attributes human characteristics or behaviours to something that is not human, such as an animal or other entity. Some stories with anthropocentric messages are based on the idea that humans are separate from and superior to the other-than-human entities on Earth. This way of thinking – sometimes referred to as "human exceptionalism" – works against the wellbeing of both children and the environment. What's needed, instead, is a worldview that appreciates the "interconnected relationality among people, land, and more-than-human beings" (op de Beeck 2018, p. 1). Also needed is the understanding that, while humans are "an exceptional and unique species … so too are all others" (Bekoff 2014, p. 19).

Anthropomorphism need not be rejected entirely as an avenue for enhancing children's relationship with animals. As noted by a number of scholars, "anthropomorphism can both help and hinder one's ability to accurately empathize with others. When true similarities are found with animals, anthropomorphism can help people better understand or empathize with the animal" (Young et al. 2018, p. 335). An important consideration relates to how the animals are depicted. Struck and Born (2024) suggest looking for "books that centre real animals, with agency and individual lives." They note how this will allow children to "see and respond to animals as sentient beings, with lives and experiences all their own" (p. 64).

The children's book *Hungry Coyote* (Blackford 2015) does this well. This book describes a year in the life of an urban coyote, who spends its time searching for food for himself and his hungry family. As noted by Struck and Born (2024), the depiction of the coyote as a competent independent creature nurtures respect and appreciation. It shows children "that animals communicate and behave in ways that are specialized, nuanced, and purposeful and that, in many cases, these behaviors happen entirely outside the human-centered world" (p. 64).

Make Way for Ducklings (McClosky 1941) is another example of a children's book that depicts a positive relationship between humans and animals without using anthropomorphism. The focus of this story is on the safety and welfare of ducks as they try to cross a busy street. The humans, in this story, go out of their way to keep the ducks safe. A policeman stops the traffic, and drivers wait patiently as the ducks cross the road to get to a pond in a city park. Making way for ducklings isn't part of the policeman's job, and spending a few minutes waiting while the ducks cross the road isn't something the drivers asked for. Yet their actions reflect being "in right relationship" with other living beings.

"Right relationship," as defined in the Earth Charter, means respecting the intrinsic value of all of nature. The concept of right relationship includes living up to an ethical responsibility based on the fact that "all beings are interdependent and every form of life has value regardless of its worth to humans" (Earth Charter 2000).

Some children's books about animals – like *Make Way for Ducklings* – give messages about the animals' need for human protection. In certain situations, this is fine. There's certainly a value in children feeling empathy for and a willingness to help animals. Some scholars, however, are suggesting that we consider a less human-centric view. Bryan Nichols (2024), for example, calls for "rational compassion" or "compassionate critical thinking" or both. He discusses ways in which empathy differs from pity, sympathy, and compassion. He also differentiates between emotional sympathy and cognitive empathy. Sympathy and emotional empathy, he says, are feelings, while "cognitive empathy is a skill-based understanding, and compassion is an action-based urge" (p. 87).

While Nichols (2024) encourages compassion as a way to reduce suffering in animals, he also cautions against focusing solely on their suffering. Messages about animals, he says, should highlight a "bidirectional flow of benefits" – that is, animals and people helping each other. Nichols highlights the importance of respect and appreciation in children's relationship with animals. "Respect," he says, "is critical and appreciation is a positive" (p. 90).

Nature – A Powerful Tool for Fostering Literacy

Literacy basically means the ability to read and write. This ability is critical for success in human society. Reading to young children is one of the most effective ways to instil an interest in reading and may encourage an interest in writing as well. Reading about nature can also promote an interest in the natural world. "Because children are curious about their surroundings, the environment provides a perfect vehicle for learning to read, write, and make sense of the world" (Kupetz & Twiest 2000, p. 59). While young children need direct experiences with the natural world to really understand and appreciate the world of nature, books can extend their understandings about nature and the way it works.

At times, nature experiences can motivate children to write and/or illustrate stories of their own. Kya, at age five, wrote a story about a mother bird who left her nest to find food for her babies. A storm made it difficult for the mother bird to get back to her nest. The mother bird knew her babies were hungry, so she flew through the wind and rain. She finally made it back and kept her babies safe. Kya's story indicates that she had some experience with birds and had developed a sense of caring about, or empathy for, other-than-human living beings. Writing the story fostered her literacy skills and, most likely, deepened her feelings about the world of nature as well.

An incident shared by an artist in a unique arts-in-nature program provides another example of nature motivating a child to write. This incident involved a child with learning and behavioural difficulties who, at the beginning of the program, refused to participate in any of the writing and drawing activities. Until the very end of the program, he made absolutely no marks on his paper. During one of the last sessions, however, he went to the garden and started to draw every single flower. He also started writing the name of each flower. This, as described by the artist, was "very big" and "amazing," as neither she nor the teacher had ever seen this child write anything before (Walshe, Perry & Moula 2023, p. 14). Perhaps he was drawing and writing about the flowers in response to the way the flowers were drawing him in.

BOX 12.1   REFLECTIONS: LEARNING FROM THE BOOK OF NATURE

Environmental education scholars, today, are encouraging us to not only learn *about* nature but also learn *from* and *with* nature. This approach, they say, should apply not only to ourselves but to our work with young children as well. They note how learning *about* nature can instil "anthropocentric and binary ideas of children existing separately from nature or the environment." These ideas reflect Western science which tends to treat nature and other-than-humans as separate entities from humans (Acharibasam & McVittie 2023). Learning *with* nature reflects a different mindset.

Learning *with* nature recognizes nature's role in the process of learning. This approach looks to nature as teacher and partner. Learning *with* nature also recognizes the reciprocity that occurs as children interact with natural elements. In learning *with* nature, children not only interact with nature but also spend time reflecting on the meaning of what they observe and experience in the natural world. It's well to keep in mind something that Albert Einstein once said: "Look deep into nature, and then you will understand everything better."

Drama and Dramatic Play as Pathways to Literacy

"Pretend" or dramatic play often involves acting out a story. The story may be about family activities at home (cooking, cleaning, etc.) or what people do for work or recreation (teaching, camping). The stories may also be about animals and how they live. Nature-themed dramatic play can encourage children to reflect on the different characteristics of the natural world and nurture kinship with animals and plants.

Dramatic play tends to occur spontaneously as a child-directed activity. A variation can also be used, at times, with some framing by adults. A theatrical performance about dying bees was used in one situation to help preschool children develop an appreciation of bees (Weldemariam 2020). Actors in bee suits presented a play about bee pollination. Children were given opportunities throughout the performance to become bee-like, to try out bee behaviour, and to enact bee concerns. This "becoming-with the bees" seemed to trigger an emotional response to the welfare of bees and promoted a sense of "response-ability" in the children.

Assessments after this experience indicated that "becoming-with the bees" impacted children's thinking and behaviour over time. Their conversations and drawings reflected an emerging sustainability mindset. Some children expressed an interest in helping to care for bees. After one child suggested planting flowers in the schoolyard, the entire class participated in the making of a flower garden for bees (Weldemariam 2020).

Other research focusing on the benefits of children taking on animal roles includes studies of children engaged in self-directed dramatic play. One such study was based on video recordings and notes taken over time in an early childhood classroom (Harju & Rouse 2018). Most of the recorded child-directed dramatic play activities involved children assuming different animal roles. The children not only referred to themselves and each other as dog, bird, deer, rabbit, and other types of animals but also actually embodied different animal characters. They were often on hands and knees, moving around on the floor and vocalizing the sounds of different animals. At times, the children used gestures and sounds to express "big" emotions, such as danger and fear. "Becoming an animal" in dramatic play reflects a relationship children feel but can't always articulate in words.

Animal stories created by children during dramatic play may reflect an important way in which children gain an embodied knowledge of nature. Children's interest in "becoming animals," for example, may reflect and nurture a sense of inter-connectedness with (rather than dominance over) the natural world. Children "becoming animals" is more effective in fostering care for animals than telling children that they should care for the other-than-human natural world. "The most well-researched method for building empathy is activating the imagination. This occurs when we engage in perspective taking through reflection, storytelling, role-playing, and mimicry" (Young et al. 2018, p. 336).

Another study involving children in caring for dying bees on their playground emphasized the need to shift environmental education with young children "from matters of fact towards matters of concern" (Nxumalo 2017). In this study, the children learned to practice stillness and slow movement while close to bees who were still showing signs of life. Some children made "offerings" to the bees in the form of flowers and sugary water. They touched the wings and "soft fur" of dead bees and provided covering for them to keep them from blowing away.

Poetry

Most young children love poetry if it's introduced to them in developmentally appropriate ways. Choosing poetry with themes familiar to children is a good place to start. Thus, poems about animals or other aspects of nature tend to work well with young children. Poems about nature can be used to promote literacy and enhance children's appreciation of the natural world.

In addition to nature-related themes, children enjoy brevity, humour, and rhyme in poetry. All three of these elements need not be present in every poem you choose, but including at least one of these elements will increase the chances of children enjoying the poem. "The Woodpecker" by Elizabeth Madox Roberts is an example of a children's poem that includes all three of these components.

> "The Woodpecker" by Elizabeth Madox Roberts
>
> *The woodpecker pecked out a little round hole*
> *And made him a house in the telephone pole.*
>
> *One day when I watched he poked out his head,*
> *And he had on a hood and a collar of red.*
>
> *When the streams of rain pour out of the sky,*
> *And the sparkles of lightning go flashing by,*
>
> *And the big, big wheels of thunder roll,*
> *He can snuggle back in the telephone pole.*

This poem, along with other poems by the same author, are in the public domain and available online. "Public domain" refers to creative materials that are not protected by intellectual property laws and thus can be used without obtaining permission. Some other nature-focused poems in the public domain that you might use with young children include the following:

- "Winter Moon" by Langston Hughes
- "April Rain Song" by Langston Hughes
- "Who Has Seen the Wind" by Christina Rossetti
- "Snow Toward Evening" by Melville Cane
- "Rain" by Robert Louis Stevenson
- "I Heard a Bird Sing" by Oliver Herford

Spiritual Literacy

In Chapter 7, I shared a personal experience about discovering that my "ecological self" and "spiritual self" aren't two separate dimensions of my identity (Box 7.1). As I write this chapter, I'm reminded of how eco-literacy and spiritual literacy overlap. Eco-literacy isn't just a cognitive ability. It integrates different forms of intelligence – emotional, social, and ecological. Eco-literacy, as described earlier, includes the "telling of the holy" (Sanders 2016) and can be recognized as a form of spiritual literacy (Binder 2011; Jirásek 2023).

A spiritually literate person is

> an individual who reflects and cultivates skills of self-reflection, who can act in relation to other people in a mode characterized by prosocial orientation and altruism, who can experience environmental sensitivity and kinship with nature, and who is capable of astonishment and amazement at experiencing transcendence in relation to the wholeness.
>
> (Jirásek 2023, p. 61)

We can see from this definition that spiritual literacy is not the same as religious literacy and can be developed in a secular environment.

Spiritual literacy in the non-religious sense cultivates four basic relationships: to self, to others, to nature, and to transcendence. Of these, the relationship with nature is most prominent in the overlap between spiritual literacy and eco-literacy. "Spirituality in relation to nature is evident in the environmental sensitivity and in the affinity with the natural world, in the possibilities of 'connection' to the landscape and the natural world" (Jirásek 2023, p. 67).

Children's literature can be used to support spiritual literacy, especially if the sharing of stories includes guided discussion. Such discussions can help children make associations between their own lives and the spiritual messages embedded in the stories. Mythological stories tend to be especially rich in embedded spiritual messages.

Spiritual literacy basically means "making meaning at a profound level." Spiritual literacy – like other forms of literacy – goes beyond reading and writing. Literacy, in this broader context, includes any form where meaning is conveyed. Unfortunately, "the current approach to literacy is predominantly print-driven, with a focus on decoding as a dominant concern" (Binder 2011, p. 22). An alternative approach is to place meaning-making at the centre of literacy. This approach to literacy empowers children to explore deeper questions about themselves and the world in which they live. This is what spiritual literacy is all about.

Conclusion

Stories can entertain and inform. They can also inspire. Stories and storytelling activities – if carefully selected – can be used to promote the spiritual dimensions of young children's connectedness to nature.

BOX 12.2   SUGGESTIONS: LITERACY OUTDOORS

The following five suggestions for fostering literacy in the outdoor environment are adapted from an article originally published in *Exchange* (Wilson 2007). These suggested activities, while fostering literacy, can also promote a deepening sense of wonder about nature and the way it works.

1. Create an outdoor literacy centre.
   Learning centres are typical features of many early childhood classrooms. They're generally designed to encourage independent learning around specific areas of development. Typical learning centres in an early childhood classroom include blocks and dramatic play, art centre, "book nook" or literacy centre, science centre, music area, and math centre. Learning centres, while generally found indoors, can be used in outdoor settings as well. A library cart might be used for moving a literacy centre from indoors to outdoors. Materials for an outdoor literacy centre might include books, maps, and field guides as well as a variety of writing and drawing materials.
2. Conduct "story time" outdoors.
   A special "gathering place" can enhance the experience of sharing stories outdoors. This place should be

conducive to both listening and discussing. While all types of books can be shared in the outdoor setting, books that focus on the local environment will have special meaning. Such books can nurture a sense of place along with a deepening appreciation of the natural world. The sharing of stories might be followed by an art activity – drawing, sculpting, painting, making a collage, and so on. Encouraging an artistic representation of what the story means can enhance children's understanding and appreciation of the story and thus be part of the meaning-making process. The sharing of stories can also be followed by guided discussion about the meaning of the story as it relates to the children's daily lives.

3. Designate a special area as an outdoor stage for live performances.

    The "stage" – while an actual platform or just a designated area – invites both impromptu and rehearsed performances of stories, poems, dances, and so on. Literacy skills involved in such performances can include recall and interpretation as well as the creation of an original story.

4. Post illustrated signs.

    Illustrated signs can be used outdoors to label elements of the natural environment (maple tree, sandy soil, prickly pear cactus, blueberry bush, etc.). Such signs can increase children's knowledge of the local environment while promoting their literacy skills. Descriptive words paired with the label ("*prickly* cactus", "*sandy* soil", etc.) can prompt closer observation.

5. Provide observational aids and recording materials.

    Rulers, measuring cups, magnifying lens, and identification cards or field guides can all be used to encourage closer observation of the natural world, along with literacy skills. Notepads, pencils, and simple illustrated checklists can motivate children to keep printed records of their observations. These observational and recording materials can prompt children to look more closely and, in the process, develop such visual perception skills as attending, discrimination, identification, classification, and categorization – all playing a role in the development of literacy skills.

Reference

Wilson, R. (2007). Nature – A powerful tool for fostering language and literacy. *Exchange, 178,* 50–60.

Afterword

There Was a Time

"There was a time ... when the world was a song and the song was exciting"—These words from the musical *Les Misérables* haunt me. They remind me of a time, very early in my childhood, when the world of nature was indeed exciting. With great fondness, I recall the scent of lilacs, the glow of fireflies, the taste of freshly picked strawberries, the feel of a baby chick's beating heart, and the sound of leaves rustling in the wind. These things I remember from my childhood days on the farm. Those days were exciting.

There was a time when most humans lived close to nature. Those days are gone. Today, more than half of the world's human population lives in urban areas—often in highly dense cities. This transition leaves many of us with only limited opportunities for direct interaction with nature. We may thus look to other less fulfilling sources for excitement and satisfaction. For children, this may mean rarely experiencing the "world as a song" and missing out on experiences that are essential for their holistic development. Wonder may be something they read about but rarely experience.

The word "wonder" appears frequently throughout the chapters in this book. At times, it's in reference to what children feel (as in a sense of wonder); at other times, it's in reference to what they do (as in pondering). "Wonder" is also used in reference to what nature has to offer. Nature is, indeed, a source of endless wonder. Yet, for most of us, that sense of wonder is dimmed or lost over time.

One of the greatest gifts we can give children is the opportunity to discover the wonders of nature and to experience the world as a song. This gift can do more for a child than any monetary gift we might offer. A sense of wonder can serve "as an unfailing antidote against the boredom and disenchantment of later years, the sterile preoccupation with things that are artificial, the alienation from the sources of our strength" (Carson 1956, p. 43).

Wonder, as an integral part of connectedness to nature, can be experienced as a dependable strength, something we can count on to shore us up when times get tough. Wonder may also be a survival skill. We usually think of survival skills in relation to what's needed to survive in the wilderness. In today's world, however, wonder may be

> the thing that helps us build an emotional connection—an intimacy—with our surroundings that, in turn, would make us want to do anything we can to protect them. It might build our inner reserves, give us the strength to turn outward and meet those challenges with grace.
> (Blake 2012, pp. ix–x)

Wonder also provides nourishment for a child's spiritual development. We can't pour spirituality into children or give them a sense of wonder. What we can do is provide opportunities for wonder to take root in a child's life. Once children experience wonder and the other "soul-making" aspects of the natural world, they'll learn to care deeply about the Earth and all the elements of the Earth. This sense of caring is perhaps the greatest manifestation of spirituality.

References

Acharibasam, J. B. & McVittie, J. (2023). Connecting children to nature through the integration of Indigenous Ecological Knowledge into early childhood environmental education. *Australian Journal of Environmental Education*, *39*, 349–361.

Adams, D. & Beauchamp, G. (2019). Spiritual moments making music in nature. A study exploring the experiences of children making music outdoors, surrounded by nature. *International Journal of Children's Spirituality*, *24*(3), 260–275.

Adams, D. & Beauchamp, G. (2021). A study of the experiences of children aged 7–11 taking part in mindful approaches in local nature reserves. *Journal of Adventure Education and Outdoor Learning*, *21*(2), 129–138.

Adams, K., Bull, R., & Maynes, M.-L. (2016). Early childhood spirituality in education: Towards an understanding of the distinctive features of young children's spirituality. *European Early Childhood Education Research Journal*, *24*(5), 760–774.

Alderton, A., Villanueva, K., O'Connor, M., Boulangé, C. & Badland, H. (2019). Reducing inequities in early childhood mental health: How might the neighborhood built environment help close the gap? A systematic search and critical review. *International Journal of Environmental Research and Public Health*, *16*(9), 1516.

Anderson, C. L., Monroy, M. & Keltner, D. (2018). Awe in nature heals: Evidence from military veterans, at-risk youth, and college students. *Emotion*, *8*(8), 1195–1202.

Argent, A., Vintimilla, C.D., Lee, C. & Wapenaar, K. (2017). A dialogue about place and living pedagogies: Trees, ferns, blood, children, educators, and wood cutters. *Journal of Childhoods and Pedagogies*, *1*(2), 1–20.

Armijo-Cabrera, M. (2025). Learning through magic? Diffractive analysis of children's experiences across post-structuralist, post-Freudian, and post-materialist perspectives. *Childhood*, *32*(2), 175–193.

Armstrong, K. (2023). *Sacred Nature*. Knoff.

Arola, T., Aulake, M., Ott, A., Lindholm, M., Kouvonen, P., Virtanen, P. & Paloniemi, R. (2023). The impacts of nature connectedness on children's well-being: Systematic literature review. *Journal of Environmental Psychology*, 85, 101913.

Arvay, C.G. (2018a). *The Biophilic Effect*. Sounds True.

Arvay, C.G. (2018b). *The Healing Code of Nature*. Sounds True.

Bai, H. (2015). Peace with the earth: Animism and contemplative ways. *Cultural Studies of Science Education*, 10(1), 135–147.

Barrable, A. (2019). Refocusing environmental education in the early years: A brief introduction to a pedagogy for connection. *Education Sciences*, 9(1), 61.

Barrable, A. (2025). Nature attachment theory: Exploring the human-nature bond through an attachment theory lens. *International Journal of Early Childhood Environmental Education*, 12(1), 64–71.

Barrable, A., Booth, D., Adams, D. & Beachamp, G. (2021). Enhancing nature connection and positive affect in children through mindful engagement with natural environments. *International Journal of Environmental Research and Public Health*, 18(9), 4785.

Barrable, A., Friedman, S. & Beloyianni, V. (2024). Nature connection in adulthood: The role of childhood nature experiences. *People and Nature*, 6, 1571–1580.

Barrera-Hernandez, L. F., Sotelo-Castillo, M. A., Echeverria-Castro, S. B. & Tapia-Fonllem, C. O. (2020). Connectedness to nature: Its impact on sustainable behaviors and happiness in children. *Frontiers in Psychology*, 11(7), 276.

Bascope, M., Perasso, P. & Reiss, K. (2019). Systematic review of education for sustainable development at an early stage: Cornerstones and pedagogical approaches for teacher professional development. *Sustainability*, 11, 719.

Beer, T., Cook, A. & Kantor, K. (2018). Running Wild: Engaging and empowering future custodians of place through creative nature-based play. *Journal of Public Pedagogies*, 3, 5–19.

Beery, T., Chawla, L. & Levin, P. (2020). Being and becoming in nature: Defining and measuring connection to nature in young children. *International Journal of Early Childhood Environmental Education*, 7(3), 3–22.

Beery, T.H. & Lekies, K.S. (2019). Childhood collecting in nature: Quality experience in important places. *Children's Geographies*, *17*(1), 118–131.

Bekoff, M. (2014). *Rewilding Our Hearts: Building Pathways of Compassion and Coexistence*. New World Library.

Bell, S.L. (2019). Experiencing nature with sight impairment: Seeking freedom from ableism. *Environment and Planning E: Nature & Space*, *2*(2), 304–322.

Binder, M.J. (2011). 'I saw the universe and I saw the world': Exploring spiritual literacy with young children in a primary classroom. *International Journal of Children's Spirituality 16*(1), 19–35.

Blackford, C. (2015). *Hungry Coyote*. Minnesota Historical Society Press.

Blake, H.E. (2012). Foreword. In *Orion Society, Wonder and Other Survival Skills* (pp. ix–x). The Orion Society.

Blenkinsop, S., Morac, M. & Jickling, B. (2022). Wild pedagogies: Opportunities and challenges for practice. In M. Paulsen, J. Jagodzinski & S.M. Hawke, *Pedagogy in the Anthropocene* (pp. 33–51), Palgrave Macmillan Cham.

Bone, J. (2008). The spiritual lens: Multiple visions of infancy. *The First Years: Nga Tau Tuatahi. New Zealand Journal of Infant and Toddler Education 10*(1), 16–19.

Bone, J. & Blaise, M. (2015). An uneasy assemblage: Prisoners, animals, asylum-seeking children and posthuman packaging. *Contemporary Issues in Early Childhood 16*(1), 18–31.

Born, P. (2024). *Multispecies Thinking in the Classroom and Beyond*. Lexington Books.

Boyd, D. (2019). Utilising place-based learning through local contexts to develop agents of change in Early Childhood Education for Sustainability. *Education 3–13*, *47*(8), 983–997.

Britanica Encyclopedia. (2024). https://www.britannica.com/topic/quality-of-life. Accessed July 21, 2024.

Broom, C. (2017). Exploring the relations between childhood experiences in nature and young adults' environmental attitudes and behaviours. *Australian Journal of Environmental Education*, *33*(1), 34–47.

Brothwell, L. (2024). Personal communication, August 19, 2024.

Buber, M. (1923/1970). *I and Thou*. Translated by Walter Kaufman. Touchstone.

Buchanan, J., Pressick-Kilborn, K. & Fergusson, J. (2021). Naturally enough? Children, climate anxiety and the importance of hope. *The Social Educator*, 39(3), 17–31.

Cagle, N.C. (2018). Changes in experiences with nature through the lives of environmentally committed university faculty. *Environmental Education Research*, 24(6), 889–898.

Cajete, G. (2001). *Native Science*. Clear Light Publishing.

Capaldi, C. A., Dopko, R. L. & Zelenski, J. M. (2014). The relationship between nature connectedness and happiness: A meta-analysis. *Frontiers in Psychology*, 5, 92737.

Carson, R. (1956). *The Sense of Wonder*. Harper & Row.

Cerino, A. (2021). The importance of recognising and promoting independence in young children: The role of the environment and the Danish forest school approach. *Education 3–13*, 51(4), 685–694.

Chang, C.C., Cox, D.T.C., Fan, Q., Nghiem, T.P.L., Tan, C.L.Y., Oh, R.R.Y., Lin, B.B., Shanahan, D.F., Fuller, R.A., Gaston, K.J. & Carrasco, L.R. (2022). People's desire to be in nature and how they experience it are partially heritable. *PLoS Biol.* 20(2), e3001500.

Chang, D. (2020). Encounters with suchness: Contemplative wonder in environmental education. *Environmental Education Research*, 26(1), 1–13.

Chatterjee, S. (2018). Children's coping, adaptation and resilience through play in situations of crisis. *Children, Youth, and Environments*, 28(2), 119–145.

Chawla. L. (1990). Ecstatic places. *Children's Environments Quarterly*, 7(4), 18–23.

Chawla, L. (1999). Life paths into effective environmental action. *Journal of Environmental Education*, 31(1), 15–26.

Chawla, L. (2007). Childhood experiences associated with care for the natural world: A theoretical framework for empirical results. *Children, Youth and Environments*, 17(4), 144–170.

Chawla, L. (2009). Growing up green: Becoming an agent of care for the natural world. *Journal of Developmental Processes*, 4(1), 6–23.

Chawla, L. & Cushing, D.F. (2007). Education for strategic environmental behavior. *Environmental Education Research*, 13(4) 437–452.

Checkley, K. (1997). The first seven … and the eight. *Educational Leadership*, 55(1), 8–13.

Chen, C., Yuan, Z. & Zhu, H. (2019). Playing, parenting and family leisure in parks: Exploring emotional geographies of families in Guangzhou Children's Park, China. *Children's Geographies*, 18(4), 463–476.

Christian, B. J. (2020). Attachment, nature, and the young child's felt sense of God. *Journal of Research on Christian Education*, 29(1), 47–60.

Cobb, E. (1977). *The Ecology of Imagination in Childhood*. Columbia University Press.

Coles, R. (1990). *The Spiritual Life of Children*. Houghton Mifflin Harcourt.

Colléony, A., Cohen-Seffer, R. & Shwartz, A. (2020). Unpacking the causes and consequences of the extinction of experience. *Biological Conservation 251*, 1–9.

Crawford, M.R. & Holder, M.D. (2012). Enhancing spirituality and positive well-being through nature. *International Journal of Psychology Research 7*(2), 83–108.

Cree, J. & Robb, M. (2021). *The Essential Guide to Forest School and Nature Pedagogy*. Routledge.

Davis, J. & Elliott, S. (2014). *Research in Early Childhood Education for Sustainability*. Routledge.

Davis, J., Elliott, S. & Arlemalm-Hager, E. (2024). *Early Childhood Education for Sustainability*. Springer.

de Saint-Exupéry, A. (1943). *The Little Prince*. Harcourt Books.

de Souza, M. (2016). The spiritual dimension of education—Addressing issues of identity and belonging. *Discourse and Communication for Sustainable Education*, 7(1), 125–138.

Deming, A.W. (2014). *Zoologies*. Milkweed Editions.

Deringer, S.A. (2017). Mindful place-based education: Mapping the literature. *Journal of Experiential Education*, 40(4), 333–348.

Dillard, A. (1974). *Pilgrim at Tinkers Creek*. Harper Collins.

DiSalvo-Ryan, D. (2019). *City Green*. Harper Collins.

Djernis, D., Lerstrup, I., Poulsen, E., Stigsdotter, U., Dahlgaard, J. & O'Toole, M. (2019). A systematic review and meta-analysis of nature-based mindfulness: Effects of moving mindfulness training into an outdoor natural setting. *International Journal of Environmental Research and Public Health*, *16*(17), 3202.

Duckworth, E. (2006). *"The Having of Wonderful Ideas" and Other Essays on Teaching and Learning*. Teachers College Press.

Dutcher, D.D., Finley, J.C., Luloff, A.E. & Johnson, J.B. (2007). Connectivity with nature as a measure of environmental values. *Environment and Behavior 39*, 474–493.

Earth Charter. (2000). https://earthcharter.org/wp-content/uploads/2020/03/echarter_english.pdf. Accessed February 5, 2025.

Elliot, E. & Krusekopf, F. (2018). Growing a nature kindergarten that can flourish. *Australian Journal of Environmental Education*, *34*(2), 115–126.

Elliot, E. & Krusekopf, F. (2017). Thinking outside the four walls of the classroom: A Canadian Nature Kindergarten. *International Journal of Early Childhood*, *49*, 375–389.

Elliott, S. (2025). Personal communication. (March 18, 2025).

Elliott, S. & Emmett, S. (1997). *Snails Live in Houses Too: Environmental Education for the Early Years*. Royal Melbourne Institute of Technology.

Elliott, S. & Pugh, R. (2020). Children's voices about fish and tadpoles in an Australian Pond Ecosystem: It's all about balancing and belonging. In S. Elliott, E. Arlemalm-Hagser & J.M. Davis, *Researching Early Childhood Education for Sustainability* (pp. 205–219). Routledge.

Ellyatt, W. (2024). Sustainability, spirituality and early childhood. In E. Rouse, B. Hyde & T. Eaude, *Nurturing Young Children as Spiritual Beings in a Globalized World* (pp. 89–100). Bloomsbury Publishing Plc. ProQuest Ebook.

English Standard Version Bible (1962). *Ezekiel* 36:28. Catholic Book Publishing.

Ernst, J. & Burcak, F. (2019). Young children's contributions to sustainability: The influence of nature play on curiosity, executive function skills, creative thinking, and resilience. *Sustainability*, *11*(15), 4212.

Ernst, J., McAllister, K., Siklander, P. & Storli, R. (2021). Contributions to sustainability through young children's nature play: A systematic review. *Sustainability, 13,* 7443.

Fasting, M. L. & Høyem, J. (2024). Freedom, joy and wonder as existential categories of childhood – reflections on experiences and memories of outdoor play. *Journal of Adventure Education and Outdoor Learning, 24*(2), 145–158.

Fisher, C. (2022). Trauma-informed nature therapy: A case study. *Ecopsychology, 15*(3), 214–221.

Frankl, V. E. (1959). *Man's Search for Meaning.* Beacon Press.

Frederickson, L.M. & Anderson, E.H. (1999). A qualitative exploration of the wilderness experience as a source of spiritual inspiration, *Journal of Environmental Psychology 19,* 21–39.

Fretwell, K. & Greig, A. (2019). Towards a better understanding of the relationship between individual's self-reported connection to nature, personal well-being and environmental awareness. *Sustainability, 11*(5), 21.

Gaminiesfahani, H., Lozanovska, M. & Tucker, R. (2020). A scoping review of the impact on children of the built environment design characteristics of healing spaces. *Health Environments Research & Design Journal, 13*(4), 98–114.

Gardner, H. (1983). *Frames of Mind: The Theory of Multiple Intelligences.* Basic Books.

Garrison, J., Östman, L. & Van Poeck, K. (2024). Anthropocosmism: An Eastern humanist approach to the Anthropocene, *Environmental Education Research, 30*(7), 1161–1176.

Gawande, A. (2014). *Being Mortal.* Henry Holt and Company.

Gellel, A-M. (2018). The language of spirituality. *International Journal of Children's Spirituality, 23*(1), 17–29.

Geller, L. (1982). The failure of self-actualization theory. *Journal of Humanistic Psychology, 22*(2), 56–73.

Gibson, J. J. (1979). *The Ecological Approach to Visual Perception.* Houghton Mifflin.

Giesenberg, A. (2000). Spiritual development and young children, *European Early Childhood Education Research Journal, 8*(2), 23–37.

Giusti, M., Svane, U., Raymond, C.M. & Beery, T.H. (2018). A framework to assess where and how children connect to nature. *Frontiers in Psychology, 8*, 2283.

Goldy, S.P. & Piff, P.K. (2020). Toward a social ecology of prosociality: Why, when, and where nature enhances social connection. *Current Opinion in Psychology, 32*, 27–31.

Goodenough, A., Waite, S. & Wright, N. (2020). Place as partner: Material and affective intra-play between young people and trees, *Children's Geographies, 19*(2), 225–240.

Goodliff, G. (2013). Spirituality expressed in creative learning: Young children's imagining play as space for mediating their spirituality, *Early Child Development and Care, 183*(8), 1054–1071.

Gray, C.E., Kahn, P.H., Lawler, J.J., Tandon, P.S., Bratman, G.N., Perrins, S.P. & Boyens, F. (2025). The importance of (not just visual) interaction with nature: A study with the Girl Scouts, *The Journal of Environmental Education, 56*(2), 126–143.

Hankin, C. & Hogarth, H. (2025). Becoming-wild with chalk and paintbrush: Material-multispecies moments for re-imagining environmental education pedagogies. *Australian Journal of Environmental Education 41*(2), 278–298.

Hanson, M.M. & Jones, R. (2020). The interrelationship of Shinrin-Yoku and spirituality: A scoping review. *The Journal Of Alternative And Complementary Medicine 26*(12), 1093–1104.

Haraway, D. J. (2008). *When Species Meet*. University of Minnesota Press.

Harju, M-L. & Rouse, D. (2018). "Keeping some wildness always alive": Posthumanism and the animality of children's literature and play. *Children's Literature in Education, 49*, 447–466.

Harlow, H.F., Dodsworth, R. O. & Harlow, M.K. (1965). Total social isolation in monkeys. *Psychology 54*, 90–97.

Hart, T. (2006). Spiritual experiences and capacities of children and youth. In E. C. Rhehlkepartain, P. E. King, L. Wagener, and P. L. Benson (Eds.). *The Handbook of Spiritual Development in Childhood and Adolescence* (pp. 163–178). Sage Publications.

Hattingh, L. (2024). Time to play, time to think: Meaningful moments in the forest. *European Early Childhood Education Research Journal, 32*(1), 22–33.

Haupt, L.L. (2021). *Rooted*. Little, Brown Spark.

Hay, D. (2000). Spirituality versus individualism: Why we should nurture relational consciousness. *International Journal of Children's Spirituality* 5(1), 37–48.

Hay, D. & Nye, R. (2006). *The Spirit of the Child*. Jessica Kingsley Publishers.

Hedefalk, M., Almqvist, J. & Ostman, L. (2015). Education for sustainable development in early childhood education: A review of the research literature. *Environmental Education Research*, 21(7), 975–990.

Hedlund-de Witt, A. (2013). Pathways to environmental responsibility: A qualitative exploration of the spiritual dimension of nature experience. *Journal of Religion, Nature and Culture*, 7(2), 154–186.

Heft, H. (1988). Affordances of children's environments: A functional approach to environmental description. *Children's Environments Quarterly*, 5(3), 29–37.

Heintzman, P. (2009). Nature-based recreation and spirituality: A complex relationship, *Leisure Sciences*, 32(1), 72–89.

Heschel, A. (1983). *I Asked for Wonder*. Crossroad Publishing.

Holder, M.D., Coleman, B., Krupa, T. & Krupa, E. (2016). Well-being's relation to religiosity and spirituality in children and adolescents in Zambia. *Journal of Happiness Studies*, 17(3), 1235–1253.

Hong, J., Park, S. & An, M. (2021). Are forest healing programs useful in promoting children's emotional welfare?: The interpersonal relationships of children in foster care. *Urban Forestry & Urban Greening*, 59, 127034.

Hoover, K. S. (2021). Children in nature: Exploring the relationship between childhood outdoor experience and environmental stewardship. *Environmental Education Research*, 27(6), 894–910.

Howell, A.J., Dopko, R.L., Passmore, H.-A. & Buro, I. (2011). Nature connectedness: Associations with well-being and mindfulness. *Personality and Individual Differences*, 51, 166–171.

Howell, R.A. & Allen, S. (2019). Significant life experiences, motivations and values of climate change educators. *Environmental Education Research*, 25(6), 813–831.

Hsu, S-H. (2017). Significant life experiences affect environmental action: A critical review of Taiwanese research. *Japanese Journal of Environmental Education*, 26(4), 51–56.

Humphreys, C. & Blenkinsop, S. (2018). Ecological identity, empathy, and experiential learning: A young child's exploration of a nearby river. *Australian Journal of Environmental Education*, *34*(2), 143–158.

Hyde, B. (2008). *Children and Spirituality: Searching for Meaning and Connectedness*. Jessica Kingsley.

Isen, A.M. (2000). Positive affect and decision making. In M. Lewis & J.M. Haviland-Jones, *Handbook of Emotions* (2nd ed., pp. 417–435). Guilford Press.

Ives, C.D., Abson, D.J., von Wehrden, H., Dorninger, C. Klaniecki, K. & Fischer, J. (2018). Reconnecting with nature for sustainability. *Sustainability Science*, *13*, 1389–1397.

Izenstark, D., Crossman, K. A. & Middaugh, E. (2021). Examining family-based nature activities among Latinx students: Contexts for reinforcing family relationships and cultural heritage. *Annals of Leisure Research 25*(1), 1–21.

Izenstark, D. & Ebata, A.T. (2019). Why families go outside: An exploration of mothers' and daughters' family-based nature activities. *Leisure Sciences*, *44*(5), 559–577.

Jack, G. (2010). Place matters: The significance of place attachments for children's well-being. *British Journal of Social Work*, *40*(3), 755–771.

Jimenez, M. P., Oken, E., Gold, D. R., Luttmann-Gibson, H., Requia, W. J., Rifas-Shiman, S.L., Gingras, V., Hivert, M.F., Rimm, E. B. & James, P. (2020). Early life exposure to green space and insulin resistance: An assessment from infancy to early adolescence. *Environment International*, *142*, 105849.

Jirásek, I. (2023). Spiritual literacy: Non-religious reconceptualisation for education in a secular environment, *International Journal of Children's Spirituality*, *28*(2), 61–75.

Jirásek, I., Roberson, D.N. & Jirásková, M. (2017). The impact of families camping together: Opportunities for personal and social development, *Leisure Sciences*, *39*(1), 79–93.

Johnson, B. (2002). On the spiritual benefits of wilderness. *International Journal of Wilderness*, *8*(3), 28–32.

Johnstone, A., Martin, A., Cordovil, R., Fjørtoft, I., Iivonen, S., Jidovtseff, B., Lopes, F., Reilly, J. J., Thomson, H., Wells, V. & McCrorie, P. (2022).

Nature-based early childhood education and children's social, emotional and cognitive development: A mixed-methods systematic review. *International Journal of Environmental Research and Public Health, 19*, 5967.

Kahn, P.H. Jr., Weiss, T. & Harrington, K. (2018). Modeling child–nature interaction in a nature preschool: A proof of concept. *Frontiers in Psychology, 9*, 835.

Kalafati, M., Flogaiti, E. & Daskolia, M. (2025). Enhancing preschoolers' creativity through art-based environmental education for sustainability. *Environmental Education Research, 31*(1), 46–73.

Kamitsis, I. & Francis, A.J.P. (2013). Spirituality mediates the relationship between engagement with nature and psychological wellbeing. *Journal of Environmental Psychology, 36*, 136–143.

Kaplan, S. & Talbot, J.F. (1983). Psychological benefits of a wilderness experience. In I. Altman & J.F. Wohlwill (eds.), *Behaviour and the Environment: Advances in Theory and Research* (pp. 163–203). Plenum.

Keats, J. (1819). Letter to George and Georgina Keats. https://lewisiana.nl/painquotes/keats-on-soul-making.pdf. Accessed February 17, 2025.

Keats, J. (n.d.) Ode on a Grecian Urn. http://www.bartleby.com/101/625.html. Retrieved February 4, 2025.

Kellert, S. R. (2007). Connecting with creation: The convergence of nature, religion, science and culture. *Journal for the Study of Religion, Nature and Culture 1*(1), 25–37.

Kellert, S. R. (2012). *Birthright*. Yale University Press.

Keltner, D. & Haidt, J. (2003). Approaching awe, a moral, spiritual, and aesthetic emotion. *Cognition and Emotion, 17*(2), 297–314.

Kemple, K. M. & Johnson, C. A. (2002). From the inside out: Nurturing aesthetic response to nature in the primary grades. *Childhood Education, 78*(4), 210–218.

Kiewra, C. & Veselack, E. (2016). Playing with nature: Supporting preschoolers' creativity in natural outdoor classrooms. *The International Journal of Early Childhood Environmental Education, 4*(1), 70–95.

Kimmerer, R. W. (2013). *Braiding Sweetgrass*. Milkweed Editions.

Kimmerer, R. W. (2024). *The Serviceberry*. Scribner.

King, H., García-Rosell, J. & Noakes, S. (2020). Promoting children-nature relations through play-based learning in ecotourism sites. *Journal of Teaching in Travel & Tourism*, *20*(3), 190–201.

Kinley, J. & Elliott, S. (2024). Sustainability starts with infants and toddlers. *Every Child Magazine*, *30*(4), 26–27.

Kline, S. (2023). Haptic rapport: More-than-human movement, sensing, and communion in US forest service trails, *Leisure Studies*, *43*(2), 263–277.

Konerman, R., Elliott, S., Pugh, R., Luthy, T. & Carr, V. (2021). Children's agency and action in nature preschool: A tale of two programs. *Children, Youth and Environments*, *31*(2), 139–150.

Kuh, L. P., Ponte, I. & Chau, C. (2013). The impact of a natural playscape installation on young children's play behaviors. *Children, Youth and Environments*, *23*(2), 49–77.

Kupetz, B.N. & Twiest, M.M. (2000). Nature, literature, and young children: A natural combination. *Young Children*, *55*(1) 59–63.

Lam, L-W., Kahn, P.H. Jr. & Weiss, T. (2023). Children in Hong Kong interacting with relatively wild nature (vs. domestic nature) engage in less dominating and more relational behaviors, *Environmental Education Research*, *29*(9), 1294–1309.

Leal Filho, W.L., Salvia, A.L., Ulluwishewa, R., Abubakar, I.R., Mifsud, M., LeVasseur, T.J., Correia, V., Consorte-McCrea, A., Paco, A., Fritzen, B., Ray, S., Gordon, N., Luetz, J.M., Borsari, B., Venkatesan, M., Mukul, S.A., Carp, R.M., Begum, H. Nunoo, K. et al. (2022). Linking sustainability and spirituality: A preliminary assessment in pursuit of a sustainable and ethically correct world. *Journal of Cleaner Production*, *380*, 135091.

Leather, M. (2018). A critique of 'forest school' or something lost in translation. *Journal of Outdoor and Environmental Education 21*(1), 5–18.

Lenz Taguchi, H. (2010). *Going Beyond the Theory/practice Divide in Early Childhood Education: Introducing an Intra-Active Pedagogy*. Routledge.

Leopold, A. (1949/1986). *A Sand County Almanac*. Ballentine Books.

Lerstrup, I., Chawla, L. & Heft, H. (2021). Affordances of small animals for young children: A path to environmental values of care. *International Journal of Early Childhood Environmental Education*, *9*(1), 58–76.

Lerstrup, I. & Refshauge, A.D. (2016). Characteristics of forest sites used by a Danish forest preschool. *Urban Forestry & Urban Greening*, *20*(1), 387–396.

Lincoln, V. (2000). Ecospirituality—A pattern that connects. *Journal of Holistic Nursing 18*(3), 227–244.

Lindgren, T. (2020). The figuration of the posthuman child. *Discourse: Studies in the Cultural Politics of Education 41*(6), 914–925.

Lindstorm, C. & Goade, M. (2021). *We Are the Water Protectors*. Roaring Brook Press.

Linzmayer, C. D., Halpenny, E. A. & Walker, G. J. (2014). A multidimensional investigation into children's optimal experiences with nature. *Landscape Research*, *39*(5), 481–501.

Lithoxoidou, L.S., Georgopoulos, A.D., Dimitriou, A. T. & Xenitidou, S.C. (2017). "Trees have a soul too!" Developing empathy and environmental values in early childhood. *The International Journal of Early Childhood Environmental Education*, *5*(1), 68–88.

Lloyd, A., Truong, S. & Gray, T. (2018). Place-based outdoor learning: More than a drag and drop approach. *Journal of Outdoor and Environmental Education*, *21*, 45–60.

Loebeck, J. & Cox, A. (2020). Tool for Observing Play Outdoors (TOPO): A new typology for capturing children's play behaviors in outdoor environments. *International Journal of Environmental Research and Public Health 17*(15) 1–34.

Louv, R. (2006). *Last Child in the Woods*. Algonquin Books.

Luchs, A. & Fikus, M. (2013). A comparative study of active play on differently designed playgrounds. *Journal of Adventure Education and Outdoor Learning*, *13*(3), 206–222.

Lumber, R., Richardson, M. & Sheffield, D. (2017). Beyond knowing nature: Contact, emotion, compassion, meaning, and beauty are pathways to nature connection. *PLoS One*, *12*(5), e0177186.

Manjeera, C., Gundu, S.R. & Rao, C.M. (2024). The role of creativity in self development. *Galaxy International Interdisciplinary Research Journal*, *12*(2), 369–373. Retrieved from https://internationaljournals.co.in/index.php/giirj/article/view/5256. Accessed February 15, 2025.

Margoni, F. & Surian, L. (2017). The emergence of sensitivity to biocentric intentions in preschool children. *Journal of Environmental Psychology*, *52*, 37–42.

Marinoff, L. (2000). *Plato, Not Prosac!* Quill Publishers.

Maslow, A. (1954). *Motivation and Personality*. Harper & Brothers.

Maslow, A. (1962). Lessons from the peak. *Journal of Humanistic Psychology 2*(1), 9–18.

Maslow, A. (1971). *The Farther Reaches of Human Nature*. Penguin.

Mata-McMahon, J. (2019). Finding connections between spirituality and play for early childhood education. *International Journal of Children's Spirituality*, *24*(1), 44–57.

Mata-McMahon, J., Haslip, M. J. & Schein, D. L. (2018). Early childhood educators' perceptions of nurturing spirituality in secular settings. *Early Child Development and Care*, *189*(14), 2233–2251.

Mata-McMahon, J., Haslip, M.J. & Schein, D.L. (2020). Connections, virtues, and meaning-making: How early childhood educators describe children's spirituality. *Early Childhood Education Journal*, *65*, 657–669.

Mathers, B. & Brymer, E. (2022). The power of a profound experience with nature: Living with meaning. *Frontiers in Psychology*, *13*, 764224.

Matthews, F. (1994). *The Ecological Self*. Routledge.

Mattsson, M., Fernee, C. R., Pärnänen, K. & Lyytinen, P. (2022). Restoring connectedness in and to nature: Three Nordic examples of recontextualizing family therapy to the outdoors. *Frontiers in Psychology*, 13, 768614.

Mayer, F. S. & Frantz, C. M. (2004). The Connectedness to Nature Scale: A measure of individuals' feeling in community with nature. *Journal of Environmental Psychology*, *24*(4), 503–515.

McCarty, M. (2006). *Little Big Minds*. Tarcher/Penguin.

McClain, C. & Vandermaas-Peeler, M. (2016). Outdoor explorations with preschoolers: An observational study of young children's developing relationship with the natural world. *International Journal of Early Childhood Environmental Education*, *4*(1), 37–53.

McClosky, R. (1941). *Make Way for Ducklings*. Puffin Books.

Miller, L. (2016). *The Spiritual Child*. Picador Publishing.

Mische, P. & Harris, I. (2008). Environmental peacemaking, peacekeeping, and peacebuilding. In M. Bajaj (Ed.). *Encyclopedia of Peace Education*. Columbia University.

Monroy, M. & Keltner, D. (2023). Awe as a pathway to mental and physical health. *Perspectives on Psychological Science*, 18(2) 309–320.

Montessori, M. (1972). *The Secret of Childhood*. (M. J. Costelloe, Trans.). Ballantine.

Montessori, M. (1986). *The Discovery of the Child*. Pierson Publishing.

Morrissey, A-M., Scott, C. & Rahimi, M. (2017). A comparison of sociodramatic play processes of preschoolers in a naturalized and a traditional outdoor space. *International Journal of Play*, 6(2), 177–197.

Moula, Z., Palmer, K. & Walshe, N. (2022). A systematic review of arts-based interventions delivered to children and young people in nature or outdoor spaces: Impact on nature connectedness, health and wellbeing. *Frontiers in Psychology*, 13, 858781.

Moula, Z., Walshe, N. & Lee, E. (2023). "It was like I was not a person, it was like I was the nature": The impact of arts-in-nature experiences on the wellbeing of children living in areas of high deprivation. *Journal of Environmental Psychology*, 90, 102072.

Muthukrishnan, R. & Kelly, J.E. (2017). Depictions of sustainability in children's books. *Environment, Development and Sustainability* 19(3), 955–970.

Nadkarni, N. (2008). *Between Earth and Sky*. University of California Press.

Nedovic, S. & Morrissey, A. (2013). Calm, active and focused: Children's responses to an organic outdoor learning environment. *Learning Environments Research*, 16(2), 281–295.

Newberg, A.B. & Newberg, S.K. (2006). A neuropsychological perspective on spiritual development. In E. C. Rhehlkepartain, P. E. King, L. Wagener, and P. L. Benson (Eds.). *The Handbook of Spiritual Development in Childhood and Adolescence* (pp. 183–196). Sage Publications.

Nguyen, L. & Walters, J. (2024). Benefits of nature exposure on cognitive functioning in children and adolescents: A systematic review and meta-analysis. *Journal of Environmental Psychology*, 96, 102336.

Nichols, B.H. (2024). Pathways to better relationships with wildlife: Clarifying concepts and considering possibilities. In P. Born (Ed.), *Multispecies Thinking in the Classroom and Beyond* (pp. 85–96). Lexington Books.

Nxumalo, F. (2017). Stories for living on a damaged planet: Environmental education in a preschool classroom. *Journal of Early Childhood Research*, 16(2), 148–159.

Nxumalo, F. & Pacini-Ketchabaw, V. (2017). "Staying with the trouble" in child-insect-educator common worlds. *Environmental Education Research*, 23(10), 1414–1426.

Nye, R. & Hay, D. (1996). 'Identifying children's spirituality: How do you start without a starting point'. *British Journal of Religious Education* 18(3), 144–154.

O'Gorman, L. (2024). "It's the only world we've got." Children's responses to Chris Jordan's images about SDG 14: Life below water. *Australian Journal of Environmental Education* 40(4), 693–705

op de Beeck, N. (2018). Children's ecoliterature and the new nature study. *Children's Literature in Education*, 49, 73–85.

Orion Society (2012). *Wonder and Other Survival Skills*. The Orion Society.

Orr, D. (1994). *Earth in Mind: On Education, Environment, and the Human Prospect*. Island Press.

Orr, D. (2002). Four challenges of sustainability. *Conservation Biology* 16(6), 1457–1460.

Pacini-Ketchabaw, V., Taylor, A. & Blaise, M. (2016). De-centring the human in multispecies ethnographies. In C.A. Taylor & C. Hughes *Posthuman Research Practices in Education* (pp. 149–167). Palgrave Macmillan.

Panzini, R. G., Mosqueiro, B. P., Zimpel, R. R., Bandeira, D. R., Rocha, N. S. & Fleck, M. P. (2017). Quality-of-life and spirituality. *International Review of Psychiatry*, 29(3), 263–282.

Parr, M.J. (2024). https://www.amazon.com/Backyard-Bird-Chronicles-Amy-Tan/dp/0593536134. Accessed February 4, 2025.

Payne, P.G. & Wattchow, B. (2009). Phenomenological deconstruction, slow pedagogy, and the corporeal turn in wild environmental/outdoor education. *Canadian Journal of Environmental Education*, 14, 15–32.

Persson, K., Andrée, M. & Caiman, C. (2024). Making kin in the forest: Explorations of ecological literacy through contemplative practices in a Swedish folk high school. *Environmental Education Research*, *30*(8), 1247–1262.

Piersol, L. (2015). Eco care: Nurturing possibility and resistance within education. PhD dissertation. Simon Fraser University. (http://summit.sfu.ca/item/16055).

Pollitt, J., Blaise, M. & Rooney, T. (2021). Weather bodies: Experimenting with dance improvisation in environmental education in the early years, *Environmental Education Research*, *27*(8), 1141–1151.

Pramling, N. & Pramling Samuelsson, I. (2025). Engaging children in what-if thinking through read-aloud conversations in early childhood education for sustainability, *European Early Childhood Education Research Journal*, *33*(2), 211–222.

Pringle, G., Boddy, J., Slattery, M. & Harris, P. (2023). Adventure therapy for adolescents with complex trauma: A scoping review and analysis. *Journal of Experiential Education*, *46*(4), 433–454.

Prins, J., van der Wilt, F., van der Veen, C. & Hovinga, D. (2022). Nature play in early childhood education: A systematic review and meta ethnography of qualitative research. *Frontiers in Psychology*, *13*, 995164.

Puhakka, R., Rantala, O., Roslund, M.I., Rajaniemi, J., Laitinen, O.H., Sinkkonen, A. & ADELE Research Group (2019). Greening of daycare yards with biodiverse materials affords well-being, play and environmental relationships. *International Journal of Environmental Research and Public Health*, *16*(16), 2948.

Putra, I.G.N.E., Astell-Burt, T., Cliff, D.P., Vella, S.A., John, E.E. & Feng, X. (2020). The relationship between green space and prosocial behaviour among children and adolescents: A systematic review. *Frontiers in Psychology*, *11*, 859.

Pyle, R.M. (1993). *The Thunder Tree: Lessons from an Urban Wildland*. Houghton Mifflin.

Ramsden, R., Pike, I., Thorne, S. & Brussoni, M. (2025). Children's outdoor play at early learning and child care centres: Examining the impact of environmental play features on children's play behaviour, *medRxiv*. https://www.medrxiv.org/content/10.1101.2025.01.21.25320884v1#:~:text=This%20study%20aims%20to%20understand%20the%20association%20between,play%20spaces%2C%20through%20the%20behaviour%20patterns%20of%20children. Accessed February 20, 2025.

Rantala, O. & Puhakka, R. (2020). Engaging with nature: Nature affords well-being for families and young people in Finland. *Children's Geographies*, *18*(4), 490–503.

Razani, N., Morshed, S., Kohn, M.A., Wells, N.W., Thompson, D., Alqassari, M., Agodi, A. & Rutherford, G.W. (2018). Effect of park prescriptions with and without group visits to parks on stress reduction in low-income parents: SHINE randomized trial. *PLoS One*, *13*(2), e0192921.

Richardson, M., Dobson, J., Abson, D. J., Lumber, R., Hunt, A., Young, R. & Moorhouse, B. (2020). Applying the pathways to nature connectedness at a societal scale: A leverage points perspective. *Ecosystems and People*, *16*(1), 387–401.

Richardson, M., Hamlin, I., Elliott, L.R. & White, M.P. (2022). Country-level factors in a failing relationship with nature: Nature connectedness as a key metric for a sustainable future. *Ambio*, *51*(11), 2201–2213.

Richardson, M. & Sheffield, D. (2017). Three good things in nature: Noticing nearby nature brings sustained increases in connection with nature. *Psyecology*, *8*(1), 1–32.

Robinson, C. (2022). The potential of 'wonder' to engage children's spirituality: It's so much more than pondering. *International Journal Of Children's Spirituality 27*(3–4), 158–175.

Rodenburg, J. & Dueck, C. (2025). *The Wild Path Home*. New Society Publishers.

Roehlkepartain, E.C., Benson, P.L., King, P.E. & Wagner, L.M. (2006). Spiritual development in childhood and adolescence: Moving to the scientific mainstream. In E.C. Roehlkepartain, P. E. King, L. Wagener & P. L. Benson (Eds.). *The Handbook of Spiritual Development in Childhood and Adolescence* (pp. 1–15). Sage Publications.

Rooney, T. (2018). Weather worlding: Learning with the elements in early childhood. *Environmental Education Research*, *24*(1), 1–12.

Roszak, T. (1992). *The Voice of the Earth*. Phanes Press.

Rouse, E. & Hyde, B. (2024). Enacting a spiritual pedagogy in the early years: Phenomenological reflections on thoughtfulness in practice. *European Early Childhood Education Research Journal*, *32*(5), 739–751.

Rumi, J. (1997). *The Essential Rumi*. HarperOne.

Ruokonen, I. & Lepisto, J. (2024). Children's artistic expressions inspired by nature during early childhood garden pedagogy. *International Journal of Education through Art*, *20*(2), 167–182.

Ryff, C. D. (2021). Spirituality and well-being: Theory, science, and the nature connection. *Religions*, *12*: 914.

Sahni, P. & Kumar, J. (2021). Exploring the relationship of human–nature interaction and mindfulness: A cross-sectional study. *Mental Health, Religion & Culture 24*(5), 450–462.

Salmon, J. (2000). Kincentric ecology: Indigenous perceptions of the human-nature relationship. *Ecological Applications*, *10*(5), 1327–1332.

Sanders, S. R. (2016). Telling the holy. In Orion (Ed.), *Wonder and Other Survival Skills* (pp. 2–22). Orion.

Sanson, A.V., Van Hoorn, J. & Burke, S.E.L. (2019). Responding to the impacts of the climate crisis on children and youth. *Child Development Perspectives*, *13*(4), 201–207.

Scartazza, A., Mancini, M.L., Proietti, S., Moscatello, S., Mattioni, C., Costantini, F., Di Baccio, D., Villani, F. & Massacci, A. (2020). Caring local biodiversity in a healing garden: Therapeutic benefits in young subjects with autism. *Urban Forestry & Urban Greening*, *47*, 126511

Schein, D. (2014). Nature's role in children's spiritual development. *Children, Youth and Environment*, *24*(2), 78–101.

Schein, D. (2018). *Inspiring Wonder, Awe, and Empathy*. Redleaf Press.

Schirp, J. & Vollmar, M. (2013). Nature, adventure and early education: A regional approach in Germany. In S. Knight (Ed.), *International Perspectives on Forest School* (pp. 27–40). Sage Publications.

Schultz, P. W. (2002). Inclusion with nature: The psychology of human-nature relations. In P. Schmuck & W. P. Schultz (Eds.), *Psychology of Sustainable Development* (pp. 61–78). Springer.

Sebba, R. (1991). The landscapes of childhood — The reflection of childhood's environment in adult memories and in children's attitudes. *Environment and Behavior*, *23*(4), 395–422.

Sendeck, M. (1963). *Where the Wild Things Are*. Harper & Rowe.

Shiota, M. N., Keltner, D. & Mossman, A. (2007). The nature of awe: Elicitors, appraisals, and effects on self-concept. *Cognition and Emotion*, *21*(5), 944–963.

Shultz, P. W. (2002). Inclusion with nature: The psychology of human–nature relations. In P. Schmuck & W. P. Schultz (Eds.), *Psychology of Sustainable Development* (pp. 61–78). Kluwer Academic Publishers.

Sideris, L.H. (2017). *Consecrating Science: Wonder, Knowledge, and the Natural World*. University of California Press.

Smith, C.S., DeMattia, E.A., Albright, E., Bromberger, A.F., Hayward, O.G., Mackinson, I.J., Mantell, S.A., McAdoo, B.G., McAfee, D., McCollum, A., Paxton, A.B., Roderer, A., Stevenson, K., Vidra, R.L. & Zhao, Z. (2025). Beyond despair: Leveraging ecosystem restoration for psychosocial resilience. *Proceedings of the National Academy of Sciences*, *122*(2), e2307082121.

Soga, M. & Gaston, K.J. (2016). Extinction of experience: The loss of human–nature interactions. *Frontiers in Ecology and the Environment*, *14*(2), 94–101.

SOL Forest School. (n.d.). https://www.solforestschool.com/. Accessed August 15, 2024.

Stavely, J. (2024). Personal communication.

Stevens, S. (2024). Personal communication.

Storli, R. & Sandseter, E.B.H. (2019). Children's play, well-being and involvement: How children play indoors and outdoors in Norwegian early childhood education and care institutions. *International Journal of Play*, *8*(1), 65–78.

Struck, M. & Born, P. (2024). Supporting children's ecoliteracy and multispecies relations through critical literacy practices: Using environmental literature in the elementary classroom. In P. Born (Ed.), *Multispecies Thinking in the Classroom and Beyond* (pp. 57–70). Lexington Books.

Szczytko, R., Stevenson, K.T., Peterson, M.N. & Bondell, H. (2020). How combinations of recreational activities predict connection to nature among youth. *The Journal of Environmental Education*, *51*, 462–476.

Tan, A. (2024). *The Backyard Bird Chronicles*. Knopf.

Tanner, R.T. (1980). A new research area in environmental education: Significant life experiences. *The Journal of Environmental Education*, *11*(4), 20–24.

Taylor, A. & Pacini-Ketchabaw, V. (2016). Kids, raccoons, and roos: Awkward encounters and mixed affects. *Children's Geographies*, *15*(2), 131–145.

Taylor, B. (2020). Dark green religion: A decade later. *Journal for the Study of Religion, Nature and Culture 14*(4), 496–510.

Templeton, J.L. & Eccles, J.S. (2006). The relation between spiritual development and identity processes. In E. C. Roehlkepartain, P. E. King, L. Wagener, and P. L. Benson (Eds.). *The Handbook of Spiritual Development in Childhood and Adolescence* (pp. 252–265). Sage Publications.

Thiermann, U.B. & Sheate, W.R. (2021). The way forward in mindfulness and sustainability: A critical review and research agenda. *Journal of Cognitive Enhancement*, *5*, 118–139.

Thoma, M. V., Rohleder, N. & Rohner, S. L. (2021). Clinical Ecopsychology: The mental health impacts and underlying pathways of the climate and environmental crisis. *Frontiers in Psychiatry*, *12*, 675936.

Thompson, J. (2022). Awe narratives: A mindfulness practice to enhance resilience and wellbeing. *Frontiers in Psychology*, *13*, 840944.

Tolle, E. (2005). *A New Earth*. Penguin.

Touloumakos, A. K. & Barrable, A. (2020). Adverse childhood experiences: The protective and therapeutic potential of nature. *Frontiers in Psychology*, *11*, 1–9.

Tsevreni, I. & Tigka, A. (2018). Young children claiming their connection with nonhuman nature in their schoolground. *Children, Youth and Environments 28*(1), 119–127.

UNESCO. (n.d.). https://www.unesco.org/en/articles/what-you-need-know-about-unescos-recommendation-education-peace-human-rights-and-sustainable. Accessed September 13, 2024.

United Nations. (1989). Convention on the Rights of the Child, United Nations General Assembly. Report 44/25.5 December, 1989.

Unsworth, S., Palicki, S.K. & Lustig, J. (2016). The impact of mindful meditation in nature on self-nature interconnectedness. *Mindfulness*, *7*, 1052–1060.

Van Gordon, W., Shonin, E. & Richardson, M. (2018). Mindfulness and nature. *Mindfulness*, *9*, 1655–1658.

van Heel, B. F., van den Born, R. J. G. & Aarts, N. (2023). Nature experiences in childhood as a driver of connectedness with nature and action for nature: A review. *Ecopsychology*, *15*(4), 354–367.

Vinning, J., Merrick, M.S. & Price, E.A. (2008). The distinction between humans and nature: Human perceptions of connectedness to nature and elements of the natural and unnatural. *Human Ecology Review*, *15*(1), 1–11.

Wagenfeld, A. & Kennedy, C. (2024). *The Nature of Inclusive Play*. Routledge.

Wagenfeld, A. & Marder, S. (2024). *Nature-Based Allied Health Practice*. Jessical Kingsley.

Wals, A.E.J. (2017). Sustainability by default: Co-creating care and relationality through early childhood education. *International Journal of Early Childhood*, *49*, 155–164.

Walshe, N., Perry, J. & Moula, Z. (2023). Eco-capabilities: Arts-in-nature for supporting nature visibilisation and wellbeing in children. *Sustainability*, *15*, 12290.

Wang, C-L. (2017). No-self, natural sustainability and education for sustainable development, *Educational Philosophy and Theory*, *49*(5), 550–561.

Wang, X., Geng, L., Zhou, K., Ye, L., Ma, Y. & Zhang, S. (2016). Mindful learning can promote connectedness to nature: Implicit and explicit evidence. *Consciousness and Cognition*, *44*, 1–7.

Ward Thompson, C., Aspinall, P. & Montarzino, A. (2008). The childhood factor - Adult visits to green places and the significance of childhood experience. *Environment and Behavior*, *40*(1), 111–143.

Warden, C. (2011). Offering rich experiences – Contexts for play, exploration and talk. In J. White (Ed.), *Outdoor Provision in the Early Years* (pp. 68–75). Sage Publications.

Warden, C. (2015). *Learning with Nature*. SAGE Publications.

Weldemariam, K., (2020). 'Becoming-with bees': Generating affect and response-abilities with the dying bees in early childhood education. *Discourse: Studies in the Cultural Politics of Education*, *41*(3), 391–406.

Weldermariam, K. & Wals, A. (2020). From autonomous child to a child entangled within an agentic world. In S. Elliott, E. Arlemalm-Hagser & Davis, J.M. *Researching Early Childhood Education for Sustainability*. Routledge.

White, P.R. (2011). A phenomenological self-inquiry into ecological consciousness. *Ecopsychology, 3*(1), 41–50.

Williams, C.C. & Chawla, L. (2016). Environmental identity formation in nonformal environmental education programs. *Environmental Education Research, 22*(7), 978–1001.

Williams, J.A., Palmer, N., Schwadel, P. & Meyler, D. (2012). The human-environment dialog in award-winning children's picture books. *Sociological Inquiry, 82*(1), 145–159.

Williams, K. & Harvey, D. (2001). Transcendent experience in forest environments, *Journal of Environmental Psychology 21*, 249–260.

Williams, T.T. (2008). *Finding Beauty in a Broken World*. Pantheon Books.

Wills, R. (2025). *Nature, Spirituality, and Early Childhood Education*. Routledge.

Wilson, E.O. (1992). *The Diversity of Life*. Belknap Press of Harvard University Press.

Wilson, E. O. (2006). *The Creation*. W.W. Norton & Company.

Wilson, R. (2007). Nature – A powerful tool for fostering language and literacy. *Exchange, 178*, 50–60.

Wilson, R. (2008). *Nature and Young Children*. Routledge.

Wilson, R. (2009). The color green: A "go" for peace education. *Exchange, 187*, 40–43.

Wilson, R. (2016). *Learning is in Bloom*. Gryphon House.

Wilson, R. (2018). *Nature and Young Children* (3rd ed.) Routledge.

Wilson, R. (2020). Why sustainability is an early childhood issue. *Exchange, 252*, 16–21.

Wilson, R. (2022). *Naturally Inclusive*. Gryphon House.

Wilson, R. & Schein, D. (2017). Supporting the spiritual development of young children. *Exchange, 234*, 26–30.

Wishart, L., Cabezas-Benalcázar, C., Morrissey, A-N. & Versace, V.L. (2019). Traditional vs naturalised design: A comparison of affordances and physical activity in two preschool playscapes. *Landscape Research, 44*(8), 1031–1049.

Young, A., Khalil, K.A. & Wharton, J., (2018). Empathy for animals: A review of the existing literature. *Curator: The Museum Journal, 61*(2), 327–343.

Young, T.C. (2024). Imagining spaces of huma(an)imality by animalizing childhoods and socializing animalhoods. In P. Born (Ed.), *Multispecies Thinking in the Classroom and Beyond* (pp. 11–28). Lexington Books.

Yurdakul, Y., Beyazit, U. & Ayhan, A.B. (2025). The effect of dialogic book reading on preschool children's perspective taking skills. *Early Childhood Education Journal, 53*, 49–62.

Zamani, Z. (2016). 'The woods is a more free space for children to be creative; their imagination kind of sparks out there': Exploring young children's cognitive play opportunities in natural, manufactured and mixed outdoor preschool zones. *Journal of Adventure Education and Outdoor Learning, 16*(2), 172–189.

Zeni, M., Schnellert, L. & Brussoni, M. (2023). "We do it anyway": Professional identities of teachers who enact risky play as a framework for education outdoors. *Journal of Outdoor and Environmental Education, 26*, 341–358.

Zylstra, M.J., Knight, A.T., Esler, K.J. & Le Grange, L.L.L. (2014). Connectedness as a core conservation concern: An interdisciplinary review of theory and a call for practice. *Springer Science Reviews, 2*(1), 119–143.

For Product Safety Concerns and Information please contact our EU representative GPSR@taylorandfrancis.com
Taylor & Francis Verlag GmbH, Kaufingerstraße 24, 80331 München, Germany